T0354729

SWORN TO SILENCE IN THE APPALACHIANS

SWORN TO SILENCE IN THE APPALACHIANS

LEE COSPER

ARCHWAY
PUBLISHING

Archway Publishing books may be ordered through booksellers or by contacting:

Archway Publishing
1663 Liberty Drive
Bloomington, IN 47403
www.archwaypublishing.com
844-669-3957

ISBN: 978-1-6657-5866-6 (sc)
ISBN: 978-1-6657-5867-3 (hc)
ISBN: 978-1-6657-5868-0 (e)

Library of Congress Control Number: 2024906385

Print information available on the last page.

Archway Publishing rev. date: 05/13/2024

"LEFT IN THE MORNING"

First, I loved my mom and dad. They were my parents, and I did my best to respect them.

I was born in a small hospital in the Appalachian Mountains in the early nineteen forties. My mother said she was walking on a road back to her parents when she first met my dad. He was dressed in a suit and tie and driving a new Model A Ford. He offered her a ride home, but she declined, telling him she did not know him. He asked her where she was coming from and she said a family's home who had hired her to do washing and ironing for them one day a week, so my dad told her that maybe he would see her again out there, and she said maybe and walked on home. There were no good jobs for women in the area where she lived, and the men were coal miners. That is how it was.

One week later, on the same day, mom walked to the family's home to do washing and ironing. After work, she was walking again, and my dad came by again offering her a ride home. She conceded but told him he had to let her out before she reached her house, because her parents would not approve. He asked if he could see her again and she said yes, but she would have to walk to town to meet him because her dad would not let her go anywhere with a man. So, she told him Monday about 4 pm. They met and sat in the car on the street for about two hours talking. They continued to see each other one day a week. She would walk to town and spend two hours sitting in the car talking with him. They began to like each other very much.

She asked my dad on the seventh time they met if he was ever married and he said, "No." She said, "Good." My dad drove her near her house as usual, because her father would not let her out, and she was eighteen years old at this time. When she walked into her home, she could tell her father was breathing as if he had been running and he asked her who was that man she kissed. She said, "The man I'm going to marry." Then her father got his razor strap out and started whipping her on her back and shoulders. She pleaded with him to stop, but he would not until her back started bleeding. She said her sisters and brothers were also beaten when they did something wrong.

My mom said she knew she couldn't take this anymore and she got her clothes together; three dresses, 3 pairs of socks, the shoes she wore, and the dress she had on, and told her mother she would leave as soon as her father walked to the garden in the morning. Her mother cried, but she could not disagree with her, she was also afraid of him.

She walked to town and began window shopping and looking at things she could not afford, and an older lady she knew walked by who lived in the town and she asked mom to go into the drug store with her. They went to the soda fountain and the lady brought her an ice cream soda and a hot dog and mom had to tell her she only had seventeen cents and the lady told her she was buying for her.

Mom's father took the money she made when she worked. She said he never had a steady job. He was a handyman who built small garages and worked on commercial buildings when he could. In the summertime, her dad made the children go with him into the mountains to pick berries. They would pick them all day and he made them chew tobacco so they wouldn't eat the berries. When evening came, they would have four buckets and bring them back to town and sell them for twenty-five cents a bucket, and her dad would take the money and spend it for what was needed. The winters were rough in the mountains and my mom said she had passed to the fourth grade, but she had to quit school because the frost was so cold in November, and she had no shoes and she would run a while and squat down and her dress would cover her feet to warm them. All the people in the surrounding areas were poor. The ones who made moonshine were making money until the authorities caught them. Counties that were called "wet" sold a lot of liquor and beer to people who bought it and sold it in the dry counties (Boot Legged it). If the feds caught them, they went to jail.

In the mountains, people looked out for the "revenuers". They would raid the houses and send people to prison. Mom told us many stories about her growing up days and she did not want us to have to live like she did. She always told me to get educated so I would not have to live the way she did.

Dad asked her to marry him, and she said yes. So, he was going to take her over to meet his sister. He rented a small house and mom was staying alone in it. He had bought groceries and things they would need, and he would take her to meet his sister tomorrow.

"TUESDAY BEFORE THE WEDDING"

My father picked my mother up at the little house and they went to his sister's house. He introduced mom to his sister, and dad went outside. Mom was looking around. There were three young boys playing in the floor and a girl sitting in a chair, and the sister asked her, "Do you know these kids belong to my brother?" Mom said her heart fell to her feet and she said he never told me. His sister introduced them to her; younger boy RK was 3 years old, middle boy Pippy was 6 years old, eldest boy Herby was 9 years old, and a 12-year-old daughter.

My mom said she could not imagine having all these children and asked where their mother was. She was told that my dad had lived with the mother of the children, but never married her. Dad came to stay with his sister to work in the union mines there and he had no intentions of going back. He said the younger boy with them did not belong to him and he wanted to keep them together because the older boys wanted to be with him. The woman he was with also had a baby boy he did not know. She was with another man and dropped all the kids off to his sister while my dad was at work, and went to Baltimore, Maryland with the man she was with. She had been gone two months and she did not come back. My mother had an extremely hard decision to make. My dad came back into the house and my mom told him, "We have to talk about this."

"DISCUSSING THE CHILDREN"

My dad agreed to discuss the children with her, and she said they looked pitiful, and she felt sorry for them.

She agreed to help raise the children, and dad's sister said she would keep them until Sunday, which would be two days after they would be married.

My mom asked dad to drive her to the county courthouse where he and the other woman lived before, and she had them search the records to see if he had been married before and there were none found. She asked him why he never told her about the kids before and he said, "You never asked me, and I was afraid you wouldn't marry me if you knew."

They were married that Friday and picked up the four kids Sunday. Mom had to take responsibility for them. She also had to get them enrolled in school. She liked all of them, but the young girl was rebellious toward her and did not want to be disciplined.

Their mother came back in one year to see them and left again. She returned after my birth and picked them up and took them to a restaurant and then brought them back. The older daughter stayed in the car with her and the man. Then, the older daughter came back with a big sand rock in her hand. Mom asked her, "What are you doing?" She answered, "I come to kill your little bastard and hit it in the soft spot of its head." My mom said when she said that she knocked her down with her fist and she kept running with mom chasing her and she jumped a four-foot fence and kept running.

Mom then began to question the boys about what their mom talked about at the restaurant. The older boy, Herby, said she told him to get a big sand rock and hit the baby in the soft spot of its head and kill it. Mom asked him if he would do that and he said, "You know I wouldn't, but I told her I would, but you know better." He said she offered twenty dollars to the one that would kill me. All the boys said she is crazy. The younger one, RK, could not talk plain but said, "Me told her me would but you know me wouldn't." Mom said for two months she carried me to the spring when she got water; the boys convinced her they would not hurt me.

It was a tough life for mom. She washed clothes on a washboard and dried them on a fence in the summer, and by the fireplace in the winter.

"DAUGHTER CAN'T COME BACK"

They made it clear the older daughter could not come back to stay or they would have the authorities manage her for trying to kill me.

My dad and mom decided to move to a three-bedroom house on a hill a few miles out of town and it had two fireplaces.

The two older boys began skipping school classes and the teachers' sent notes to mom and dad and told them. Dad hit them on their butts with a belt and they stopped for a time.

Dad began drinking alcohol on the weekends and getting in poker games with men he knew and would come home drunk and with no money, and him and mom would fight over this. She would punch him in the nose and pull his hair and we were screaming; but he never hit her. He tried to hold her back.

Dad's sister told mom he drank on the weekends and worked making moonshine. He told her this when he was with the other woman. My grandpa (mom's dad) finally conceded and let dad and all the kids come to see them. Our other brothers were introduced to the grandparents and mom's dad was not happy. We ate dinner and went back home. My grandma was happy to see all the children. She was a religious lady and kind to everyone. Dad always had a good relationship with everyone, but he was not anxious to go back to my grandfather's.

We continued to live where we were as the Second World War was ending, and the mines were still on strike. We only had salt bacon in our refrigerator ("hungry") and some pinto beans. Mom was worried not knowing when the strike would end. Some neighbors traded chicken and pork meat when they had it. Everyone was running out of food. My dad was with the union in town on strike. Some of the surrounding towns with unions sent bags of basic food like lard, pinto beans, potatoes, and corn meal to the union miners. The government gave out ration stamps from the war. If you had stamps and the money, you could only buy what was on the stamps. I was crying for cocoa all the time but could not get it.

"NEEDING SOMETHING TO EAT"

My uncle who was married to mom's sister came by in a new Cadillac with Illinois plates on it and my mom asked where he got it and he said he stole it, while looking in the refrigerator. He then said, "You don't have anything to eat?" He asked if he could have a cup of coffee. Mom said we did not have any and he said, "I will be here a couple of days and I will find something." He lived with my aunt, and he went up the road where they lived. He was always writing bad checks and had been in prison several times for that; and he did not care what he had done.

"FOOD AT LAST"

Two days passed and my uncle was knocking on our door. My mom got up and let him in. He told her he had lots of groceries in the car for us. I was awake and my dad got up and asked where he got them, and he said do not worry about it. I seen several boxes of cocoa, and I was happy. My mom and dad were scared, afraid someone had seen him, and they asked him to get out, afraid the law would come to our house. My mom told me not to tell anyone about this. It was on the news that the A & P was broken into; my mom panicked, and I did not. I was happy to have cocoa!

He unloaded a lot of groceries on the kitchen table, and I thought we were rich! After he got all the food in, he said he was going back to Chicago and told us bye. He left to go back to Chicago, and we continued to struggle.

It was a long strike, and our shoes were worn out. The soles were flapping when we walked. Mom got some wire and fixed them back. They did not last long.

"STRIKE OVER"

Finally, the mining strike was over, and dad continued to drink on the weekends and gamble, playing cards. He would leave us in the car with mom and would be in a poker game and mom could not get him out of it. She could not drive and would be offered a ride home at nine or ten o'clock at night and take us home.

We were tired and sleepy and someone at the beer joint, as it was called, would buy us some chips and a pop and we would go home and have a cup of milk and go to bed to be awakened at four or five a.m. by dad coming home drunk and them fighting. This happened all the time.

"BLACK EYES AND COCK FIGHTS"

She would black dad's eyes and the men at work would ask him what happened, and he would say he run into a door, and they said we think we know the doors name, meaning my mom. My dad continued to do this and began to take us into Virginia to chicken fights on Saturdays and we wouldn't get back until three or four a.m. Sunday morning.

We sat on benches and watched the "cock fights" as they were called. They had big lights to light it up at night and people would cheer for their rooster to win. Mom was growing tired of this. Me and my younger brothers were tired, and she took us to the car. We all were sleeping as she would go back trying to get my dad to leave. He would wait until the last chicken fight before he would leave. He would be sobering up from drinking, and he and mom would argue all the way home. All the kids were happy to get home. Mom would tell me, "Don't tell anybody about this." I said OK.

My mom was tired of all the drinking and gambling, but she had nowhere to turn. She did not want to go back to her family or split the children up, so she continued to stay at home.

"ROOSTERS COMING FOR CHICKEN FIGHTS"

My dad bought him a big fighting rooster and his gambling friends bought one also. They asked dad if he would keep all of them and he said yes. They went to town and bought chicken wire and wood to build coups for the roosters to stay in at night and they made a fence around the coup so they could be out in the daytime. They paid dad a little money for chicken feed to keep them, so we had them in our back yard for a long time. Dad would go to poker games every other Friday and chicken fights every other Saturday.

It got emotional for me when he took his prize rooster to fight. They all put spurs right above their feet so they would stick each other with them, and they were bloody and would fight until one of them died. I was screaming for dad to win, and he did. It had me so scared. I did not want the rooster I had fed to die. It was in the forties and nothing much had changed. We were still poor, and mom was frustrated and still having fights with dad to buy clothes for us kids and to buy food for us.

"ELECTRIC TURNED OFF"

Another mining strike had come, and it was winter. The electric company had shut the electricity off because most people could not pay for it. My mom's brother came by to see us, and he said he was going to climb the pole by the highway and turn it back on. Dad told him not to do that as the electric man would get him in trouble, and my uncle said, "I will whip his ass if he does." My uncle left and went back home, and mom and dad told us we could not turn a light or anything on, it would get us in trouble. We didn't have much daylight because it was winter and the sun would go down behind the mountains early, so we sat by the fireplace to do our homework for school.

"NEEDING FOOD"

My confidante was my teacher. I told her everything about mom and dad fighting and she would go over to the store sometimes and buy me a carton of milk. She would let me go to the outside toilet to drink it and tell me to put the carton in the garbage at the back of the school. The milk was in a small bag. She didn't want to embarrass me. She was so good to me, and I didn't want her to embarrass me, and I loved her.

"SABLE COAT"

Dad's work strike was finally over, and we got our electric back and some food. Dad kept gambling in poker games and one night he won big! One of his big bosses from work was in a game with him and the others and he came home with seven hundred dollars and a new Sable Coat that his boss had bought his wife for Christmas. His boss ran out of money and gambled her coat to my dad in exchange for the money. Mom walked up to our school with the fur coat on and all the kids were feeling her fur coat and saying we were rich. My mom didn't have a winter coat, just a sweater, so the fur coat came in handy for her. She covered us kids up with it many times when she couldn't get dad out of the games.

Finally, the winter and the mining strikes were over, and it was spring. Many of the roosters had been replaced. Some died in the winter, and some died in chicken fights. Dad kept taking us into Virginia with the chickens, to fight with the others.

My mom was writing to her sister Edith in Baltimore, and she told mom to come stay with her for a while. She sent mom money for my younger brother Glenn, myself, and mom for bus fare.

Dad got drunk and was in a poker game and came home drunk and broke. He passed out and mom started wringing the roosters' necks and killing them on the porch. She sent word to the neighbors to come get the chickens to cook as they were just killed. I begged her to not kill them; she told me to shut up. Some of them flew up on tree limbs trying to get away from her, but chickens can't fly far, and she climbed the trees and wrung their necks and threw them down. She piled them upon the grass and stacked them on the front porch and the neighbors came and got them to cook.

Dad got up in the late afternoon and they were fighting again, and she hit him on the head with a steel fireplace poker and cut a large gash in his head and he was bleeding a lot, and a neighbor took him to the hospital. My little brother was screaming. The blood was all over the floor, and we thought our dad was dying. After a few hours, the neighbor brought him back from the hospital with a big bandage on his head and he was angry she had killed all the fighting roosters of his friends, also. She told him she couldn't live like this anymore.

Dad went to work on Monday morning and mom packed a suitcase and a shopping bag of clothes for us. We caught a taxi to the bus station, and she got tickets for us to Baltimore.

The bus looked so big to me. I had never been on one before. My brother and I did not realize we were leaving our dad and other brothers, maybe for a long time. We finally arrived at a big bus station in the city. It was dark, and mom took my aunt's address out and seen a cab driver and asked if he could take us there, and he said yes. I had never seen so many lights before. We had never been to a big city before; it was a little scary. We were hungry. We had only eaten some cookies and had a pop where the bus had stopped before. We had to change buses, and I don't remember where we changed. We were tired.

The cab driver finally stopped at a big apartment complex, and we got out. Mom took us up to the second floor and knocked on the door. My aunt greeted us. We were happy to see her. She said our uncle was working the evening shift and would be home late. She made us something to eat and put me and my brother to bed. When we woke up the next morning, our uncle was home, and he was happy to see us.

My mom got up early the next day to go look for a job. The factories were close by, and my aunt printed several names of them down and drew a map for where they were so mom could find them.

My aunt was keeping us, and her little boy was playing with us. Mom came back and she was very happy she found a job in a factory that was making war materials and something to do with ammunition. She was feeling better and helped my aunt make food and put it in the freezer so she wouldn't have to cook all the time. Mom had to work on the evening shift, 3 pm to 11 pm, all the time. My uncle sometimes worked day shift, but he mostly worked from three to eleven pm.

My brother and I began to miss our dad and we would cry and ask mom to take us home to be with our dad. She would say, "We can't go yet". We had been in Baltimore about three months, and dad was writing letters and asking mom to bring us home and promising he would quit drinking. He sent us an 8x10 picture of himself he had made at a studio, and we were crying to see him. In the meantime, my uncle had begun to stop at bars and my aunt didn't like that. He told her he would do what he wanted. Mom was told she would have to work the midnight shift for a while, and she said OKAY. She continued to work the midnight shift and got home at 7:30 am.

My uncle's boss bought a new Cadillac and he let my uncle drive it home at night and he started taking us with him to the bar at night. We would sit in a booth with them. Our aunt bought chips and a pop, and she played the jukebox for us. We liked that better than staying in the apartment.

Mom continued to come home early in the morning, and she asked our uncle not to take us in the car and be drinking, but he wouldn't listen and me and my brother were crying everyday looking at our dad's pictures and wanting to go home. My mom was trying to save enough money to get her own place, and my aunt said she would keep us if that's what she wanted. I guess it was meant to be that way.

Our uncle took the day off to get his old car fixed so he could drive it. He got it fixed and bought him some beer. My aunt cooked dinner and was getting the house cleaned up. We all ate dinner and our uncle started drinking again and mom told him not to take us out with him drinking and he said he wouldn't. Mom got ready for work, and he was still drinking. She left for work.

My uncle told me to get up and to put clothes on my brother and told my aunt to get their little boy dressed so we could go to the bar. My brother had put one of my shoes far up under the bed and I was crawling under the bed to get it. Uncle was drunk and he pulled me out from under the bed and I only had one shoe on. He wouldn't let me get the other one and told us to go get in the car and I told him I had to go pee and he said, "Piss on yourself you little bitch!" My aunt told him to stop, and he slapped her face and told us to get to the car. She was crying, and she led me out with one shoe on and one off. I told her the pee was running down my legs and she said, "It's okay, honey". She put me and my brother in the back seat, and her little boy in the front with them. Uncle was taking us to the bar and got in the wrong lane and hit a car head on, and their little boys' head hit the windshield and got a big gash in his forehead. We were all crying because he was bleeding bad and fire trucks were all around us with ambulances and police surrounding us. Blood was running down their son's face and in the car. My uncle told the police his buddy was driving, and he took off.

They put us all in the ambulance and took us to the emergency room. They pulled the white curtains around us and took my aunt's son behind another curtain to suture his head up. He came out with a big bandage around his head and me and my brother were released to my aunt. The doctor said we were okay. My uncle was so drunk he could hardly walk, and the nurse called a taxi to take us home.

My aunt put me and my brother to bed, and our uncle passed out on the sofa in the living room. My aunt was crying and kissed us good night. She took her son to bed after she made him a bottle of milk. The next morning my mom was coming home from work and her and my aunt were talking. She seen my aunt's son's head bandaged and demanded to know what happened and then she came to inspect me and my brother to see if we got hurt. She asked what happened and I told her about the accident and how my uncle was cussing me and wouldn't let me go pee and mom walked back in the living room where our uncle was on the couch, and she picked up a large Pond's Cold Crème and hit him in the forehead with it. She was screaming, "I told you not to take my kids in the car and you drinking." He was bleeding and our aunt was crying and ran into the hallway knocking on doors and one man opened his door and came out and seen all the blood and his wife said they would take him to the hospital. She got a clean towel and she put it on his head and said she would hold it there with pressure to try and stop the bleeding. They handed a very bloody towel to my aunt that the lady had put on his head and left for the hospital.

In the meantime, mom was packing our clothes quick as she could to take us back to our dad. She got our tickets and we had to wait two hours for the bus. We needed to go home to our dad. We were waiting for the two hours to go by, and she bought us some breakfast and we sat down and ate. She had coffee and a doughnut herself, and then she lit a cigarette, and she began to walk the floor at the bus station, acting as if she didn't know what to do. She said, "I hate having to leave my sister with that drunk."

Our bus finally arrived, and we were on our way back home. The trip seemed like forever. We wanted to see our dad so bad. Mom was very frustrated not knowing what to do. Soon, we were pulling into the bus station and our dad was waiting for us. Mom had sent him a telegram telling him our arrival time. We ran to our dad as soon as we seen him. He picked both of us up at the same time and we didn't want to let go of him. Mom walked up and they hugged, and we got in the car and headed for home.

We got there and our brothers were happy to see us, and we were overjoyed. Dad told mom he wouldn't be drinking, and she said she hoped not.

Dad began meeting with some of his friends that gambled, and they were shooting dice. They called it craps. Dad was losing money but staying sober. It was late winter, and my uncle came by, and we had a foot of snow, and he was in a brand-new Cadillac with Illinois tags and he came from Baltimore and left my aunt there. Mom asked, "Whose car is that?" He said, "I stole it."

There was a briefcase and a lot of legal papers and men's suits and white shirts in the car. He told my dad, "I brought these to you, and there's also two pair of shoes, and they will fit you." Dad told him he didn't want anyone else's clothes. My uncle then asked if he wanted the leather briefcase. Dad told him a coal miner doesn't need a briefcase.

Mom pulled the suits out of the car and looked at them and noticed they all had been cut off, sewn, and turned up. She said, "You have stolen a one-legged man's clothes. You are a sorry thing to do that."

Dad told him to get out of there before he gets in trouble. He tried to pull the car forward, but it was stuck in the mud and snow. He asked mom if she had anything to put under his wheel and she said no. He then said, "I do", and put the suits and shirts under his wheel and was spinning the tires for a long time, and finally got out and left those clothes there with mud on them from spinning into the ground. Mom built a fire outside and burned them and told me don't tell anyone this. I promised her I wouldn't. Mom told dad I hope he doesn't come back and told him what happened in Baltimore.

It was four days later, and my younger brother and I seen him coming back in that car. The snow had melted, and the sun was shining. He pulled into our yard and got out of the car. He was drinking, and we followed him into the house. He sat down and started talking to my dad and told him he had to get back to Baltimore and wanted to borrow money.

"DAD'S GUN"

He asked for one hundred dollars and my dad said, "You have never paid me back the hundred dollars you owe me, so I'm not loaning you anymore." Then, he ran to my mom and dad's bedroom and pulled my dad's loaded gun out of his top chest drawer, and pointed it at my dad and said, "I'll bet you will now!" My dad wrestled him down, and I was on my knees praying saying, "Please don't kill my daddy!" My brother was crying and screaming, and mom got between them, and he put the gun in her temple and was pulling the trigger and I was praying, "Please God, don't let him kill my mommy!" My brother was still screaming. The gun snapped on all the bullets and indented all of them but didn't go off. I was saying, "Thank you, God!" My dad got the gun away from him and ordered him out of the house. He left the house and mom said, "Don't come back!"

It took us all a while to calm down. I asked dad to take the gun outside and shoot it, and he said it probably won't fire, but he took it out on my insistence, and it fired on every shell. I told them God answered my prayer! They all kept looking at me all evening.

"KOREAN WAR"

We all thought things had calmed down until our oldest brother Herby was drafted to the Korean War! We were all saddened and worried about him. The cemetery was across the road on a high hill across from us and we heard many of the twenty-one-gun salutes and we knew many of the family's sons who had died in the war, and we went to several funerals. It was scary!

Dad came home from work Monday evening, and he looked sad.

Mom asked, "What's wrong?" He said, "We have to go on strike again." It scared us all. We knew what that meant. Dad was hoping it wouldn't last long.

Dad's sister and her husband came to see us. They own a grocery store in Ohio and his sister asked if our younger brother RK could go back with them; and dad asked him if he wanted to, and he said yes. I know why he said yes, "the grocery store". His mom was the woman my dad lived with, but never married. Dad asked mom what she thought about it, and she said it wasn't for her to say and we would all miss him badly, but dad's sister said she would take good care of him, so we settled in with it at the time.

The next morning, we all got up and dad's sister and her husband were getting ready to leave and she asked mom to get our brother's clothes ready. Mom got a large shopping bag and packed his clothes in it, and she put coffee on the stove and said she would make breakfast, but his sister and her husband said they would stop at a restaurant to eat. They knew we were about to cry and wanted to get out of there. They drank a cup of coffee, and our brother had a glass of milk. They were packing the car, and all of us kids were crying, and mom and dad had tears in their eyes. We were sad. We now have one big brother left. He is the one who always made us laugh and kept us happy. He also always found a little job when the strikes came. He was our favorite brother!

Dad's mining strike is continuing, and mom said we would have to give our dog away because we would have to feed it and couldn't. We were crying, and our older brother said he would work for some money so we could feed the dog. He walked to town and asked the man at the liquor store if he could do some work for him, and he said yes. He did some yard work, and the man gave him three dollars. He bought a pound of bologna, some salty crackers, and some candy bars for us. Dad still wasn't home; he was in town with the striking miners. Our brother gave us some of the bologna and crackers and we were eating so fast our little brother choked on it and mom ran her finger down his throat and he threw it up and continued eating. I threw the dog a slice of bologna. He was begging and he ate it so fast he threw it up; mom said I forgot to take the string off the slice I gave him and that's why he threw up. Mom got a stick and pulled the string out of the vomit and our poor dog ate it again after the string was out.

Days were going by, and we would be starting school again in a month, and they had signs everywhere that a carnival was coming to town. Me and my younger brother were picking pop bottles up to sell so we could go to the carnival. Dad was still on strike. We got a lot of pop bottles and sold them at our grocery store, and we had enough money to go to the carnival and it seemed like heaven to us. We were so happy our older brother got to work some more for the man at the liquor store so he could go with us. We were happy we were going tomorrow. Dad would be with the strikers again tomorrow, so we asked him to drop us off at the carnival and he said OK.

Our older brother was happy, and we got up when dad got up at eight a.m., ate breakfast and he dropped us off at the carnival and it had just opened for the day, and we all went in.

Some man was talking to our older brother and told him he would pick him up tomorrow. We thought he got a job. The man gave him five dollars and said, "I'll see you tomorrow.", and our brother said OK. We asked if we could go with him tomorrow and he said OK, as he had enough money for us, too. We got up early and got to go again. We walked a little down the road and the man our brother was talking to yesterday picked us up and drove us to the carnival and we all got out and the man got us free rides and cotton candy. When he was taking us home, he gave our brother a brown paper bag with something in it and I asked what it was. My brother said it was rocks, and I asked, for what? He said he wanted him to keep them, so don't tell anybody and I said OK. The man drove us home again and our brother told us to run ahead of him and he came in after us. We told mom the carnival man gave us a ride again and he is our brother's friend. She said we can't go to the carnival anymore; that's enough. Your older brother can go by himself; he is getting money for something. We were so happy going to the carnival.

"DYNAMITE!!"

Two days after we went to the carnival, me and my little brother were playing under the house and we saw something shiny, and we got it out from under the house. There were two packs of it, and it looked like two strings were tied to it. Mom came out and seen what we each had in our hands and was screaming, "Listen to me! Take it over there and lay it down easy, and don't drop it." She screamed at us so badly and said it was dynamite with the caps on it and that it could have blown up under the house. She asked if we had seen it before and we said no. She said she would find out where it came from. Mom told us to never tell this to anyone. We said we wouldn't.

"BROTHER DOING ODD JOBS FOR MONEY"

Our brother came home, and he had trimmed bushes for someone in town and he told mom he would go get milk and eggs from a woman who lived up the road that had cows and chickens; and sold eggs and milk. Mom told him she had to talk to him first. She made me and my little brother go into the living room. They sat at the table, and she asked him about the dynamite, and he said he is keeping it for the carnival man, and he told him to bring it back to him Friday and the man paid him five dollars to keep it until then. Mom told him that he couldn't talk to that man anymore or go around him. I think he is dangerous. Our brother said he wouldn't, and the carnival was ending on Friday.

"CARNIVAL LEAVING FRIDAY"

The week went fast, and dad turned the radio on, and the news was saying the bank vault was blown open and the money was gone. Mom said maybe it was that man, and dad said don't say something you don't know, and they quit talking about it.

We start school in a week, but we don't have any school clothes or shoes because we don't have money for them. We still have our dog, and we are happy with him. He was as skinny as us. We would hug him bye and catch the bus to school. School started, and when we came home that evening our dog wasn't there to meet us and we were looking for him and wishing for him; and we couldn't find him anywhere. I told mom and dad, "You took him away from us", and mom turned her head away from us because we were crying. We had a real bond with our dog, and he was smart. We were looking for him to come home every day. I marked the calendar off for each day he was gone, and I prayed everyday that he would come home. I kept looking out at the road where the school bus picked us up and I imagined seeing him. Finally, on the eighth day, I came home from school and marked off the calendar and went outside looking for him to come. I looked up and I seen him running toward me and I yelled for my brother and Pepper jumped into my arms and he was happy as we were. Mom just couldn't believe it. I told her you took him away, but he loved us, and he found us. She admitted they took him to another county and let him off in the mountains that were twenty-five miles away, and he found his way back. Mom said they would never do that again. God answered my prayers, and I knew he would!

Pepper was wilder after he was in the woods and started running on the highway and we couldn't stop him. Two weeks later he got killed by a car, and we were heart broken and our older brother was too. Mom said don't talk about it and our older brother buried him for us.

Some man from another county came to see dad and asked if he would run a beer joint for him and said he would buy the liquor, beer and slot machines; and we could live in the house behind it and dad asked mom and she said we have to do something. The man said you can make money to help your family.

Mom got a letter from my aunt in Baltimore and her husband went to prison again; our aunt needed money to come help them run the place, and dad gave mom money for my aunt to come. She came right away and took her little boy to our grandmother's, and she kept him. My older brother and aunt began working together at the place and business was growing.

"HAPPY TO SEE AUNT!"

The man put a big Wurlitzer jukebox on the dance floor, and it was lit up in beautiful colors of red, green, yellow and orange, and it was so pretty to us. In the back room behind the counter there was fifteen slot machines, and the man gave me and my little brother a bag of nickels, dimes, and quarters to play the slot machines and the jukebox. We were so happy! It was fun for us. Mom told our aunt that she would be having another baby in six months. My aunt said she wouldn't be able to work much after six months, and mom said that was true.

We didn't know all this was illegal. We didn't know what that word meant. We heard them talk about it. We moved into a brick sided house the man told us to live in, behind the business, and it was better for the kids. Dad told the man we have to keep our other house we rent. The man asked how much rent we paid for it and dad said twelve dollars a month. The man counted out six months of rent and handed it to dad and said pay it so there's no problem. He also said your rent is free in the house here. They turned the lights out and mom, dad and my older brother went back to the other house to get the rest of our clothes, dishes, and pots and pans. They already had moved three beds, a sofa and chairs in a big truck this morning, after the man told them we could live there. My aunt stayed with us in the beer joint and some people stopped and played the juke box and ordered some beer and some man came in and wanted to play the slot machines and our aunt had change for them. We left the house lights off and stayed in the business until they came back with everything we needed. Dad was laughing and said our aunt would be good working with them. Dad had to drive us to school every day in the county where we lived before. That's why they wanted to keep the old rental house, because our school is in that county. Mom reminded me to not talk about us moving and I said OK.

The beer joint began to get a lot of business. When someone walked in all they could see was a jukebox and a pop cooler, and a lot of chips, candy, peanuts and a counter and cash register. Everything else was in the back rooms and the customers knew to go into the back room to drink. My brother and I would dance on the dance floor and people would throw us money and we would dance for them. We had to be in bed at seven thirty every night because we had to go to school.

About 2 months after we moved in, dad's strike was over, and he went back to work on the afternoon shift. He drove us to school and had a neighbor pick us up.

Dad and mom worked the day shift in the business and our aunt and older brother worked at night. The weekends, Friday and Saturday, were very busy. People loved playing the slot machines and the man, dad's friend, added some more slot machines.

"FLOOR OF OUTBUILDING COLLAPSED WITH MOM IN IT!!"

The man came once a week to talk to dad and he said dad could draw a crowd anywhere he went. He said if they could go to a bigger city, they could get rich! Our house had seventeen hundred cases of beer stacked on the front wall and there was a little separate room from the house. It was a block cellar under the flooring of it. On the top floor were fourteen hundred cases of beer stacked on the upper floor, and they kept the cellar fully stocked and replaced the beer as it was sold. They also had cases of whiskey under the house floor.

Time was up for mom to have the baby and my aunt told her to quit lifting the beer cases, but she wouldn't listen. I seen her go to the out-building, as we called it, to get a case of beer and I ran to tell my aunt; she had told me to tell her, and she would get it. My aunt ran out the door and I was right behind her. When we got out, we heard my mother screaming and my aunt opened the door to the outbuilding, and the floor had collapsed. All we could see was my mom's head and one arm, and she was screaming. My aunt said run and get your brother, Pippy. I ran in the place and said, "Mom is stuck in the beer cases." Him and my aunt were saying, "Oh my God".

My brother crawled down in the beer cases and was lifting cases of beer off her, and she was crying saying the baby may be dead. My aunt told me to go back in the place and there was a man and a woman at the counter and people in the back playing the slot machines, and I was crying, and the man and woman asked what was wrong. I told them and they ran outside and helped get the beer cases off my mom. My aunt asked me to get a sheet off the bed and bring it to them and they folded it up length wise and handed it to mom to hold on and they pulled her out! Her leg was skinned up and bleeding and my aunt told my brother to go watch the counter and he went back in the place. My younger brother was sleeping while this took place, and he wanted to know what had happened. I told him. We were all worried about mom.

My aunt made us dinner and me and my younger brother and mom stayed in the house to eat. My aunt took plates in the beer joint with food for her and older brother to eat.

"LABOR PAINS"

I was really tired from being so scared. My aunt and my mom and brother thanked the people who helped get my mom out and my aunt gave them another beer and they left and said they would come back and play the slot machines sometime.

The next morning, we were getting ready for school and my mom was up and she had bruises all over her and said her whole body was sore. My dad got up and he told her he was sorry she got hurt and told her not to lift that beer and that she should stay in the house a few days and rest. My dad stayed up and drove us to school. He told the neighbor she wouldn't have to take us anymore. My aunt started picking us up and we were happy about that.

Mom was feeling bad four days after her accident, and she began having labor pains and they sent my aunt to get the doctor to deliver the baby. She went to town, and he followed her back. My aunt was in the house with the doctor, and she was heating a big pan of water on the stove for him, and he was trying to comfort mom. They made me leave and go back to the business, and I was hearing my mom screaming and it was taking a long time for her to have the baby. I knocked on the door and asked what was taking so long. My aunt said he had to turn the baby and told me not to come back there again. One hour later my aunt came and told us, "It's a boy. You have a baby brother." My brothers were happy, and I was also; but I wanted a sister, too many boys in the family. Dad was happy that mom was ok. We all were tired and went to bed after they closed the business. We didn't go to school the next day. We begged to stay home with baby brother and mom said we could. Our older brother and aunt were running the business and we stayed in the house with mom, and dad went to work that evening. Mom told us she would have to go to town and buy the baby some more clothes and I asked her if she would buy me a dress and my younger brother asked for a shirt and pants, and she told us she would buy us all something that we had more money since our dad was working and making money from the business. We went to school the next morning and our aunt picked us up and when we went into the house, mom had two dresses for me and two pairs of pants and two shirts for my younger brother. She also had two shirts for my older brother and two pairs of pants, and two pair of pants and two shirts for our dad; and a lot of baby clothes. She didn't buy herself anything but gave our aunt money so she could pick her own clothes. We were all happy.

It is Saturday and the man who set the business up was coming today, and dad had to give him money. I saw dad counting hundred-dollar bills, fifty-dollar bills and more money to give to the man. I asked him how much money that was, and he said, "You don't need to know and don't tell anybody this." I said OK.

The man came and I saw dad hand him all that money and the business was busy. People were playing the slot machines and drinking beer at the counter and dad took the man in our house in the back of the place and he told him how the floor of the outbuilding collapsed with my mom in it, and all the beer fell in on her, and the man said he was happy that she wasn't hurt. He told dad he would have a man over Monday to put a new floor in the outbuilding and he would put a bed and some furniture in it and dad could rent it to people. Mom told the man some of the town Harlots were coming up there with men and that was not a good idea. That man said, "Money is money!" I didn't understand what that meant, and I asked mom what it meant, and she said, "The bad women are coming to look for men up here and that's all you need to know." Mom didn't like what he said. The man went home but first he told dad to store all the beer under the outbuilding.

"BUSINESS PICKING UP"

On weekends in the business, we had standing room only. Sometimes people couldn't dance, "too crowded", but they played the jukebox, and they lined up to play the slot machines. Dad was still loaning money to his friends, and some paid him back and some didn't. Mom told my dad to put some money in the bank and he said, "We can't because they would want to know where it came from." I asked him who would want to know, and he told me I didn't need to know; and you don't want to say anything about this to anyone. I said, "I won't."

Time was passing by, and school would be out in two weeks for the summer. We would be happy and get to stay up a little longer. We were missing our old house. When we were there dad would let me and younger brother go to town with him, and we loved to stop at the beer joint the black people ran. They played the blues on the jukebox, and we would dance for them and some of them brought their babies with them, and they were so sweet. Dad knew all the men from the coal mines and grocery stores, and he liked them, and they all liked him. I never knew anyone who didn't like my dad.

My mom was loved by everyone who knew her for her kindness. She wasn't as outgoing as my dad, and she had to put up with him gambling and drinking. She tried to watch us kids as much as possible, but the baby boy took a lot of her time. My younger brother Glen would sneak into the pop coolers and get us some grape pop. There was a flowing creek beside the house with bushes by it and he would put us some grape pop in the creek at the edge to stay cold and he got a bottle opener from the kitchen drawer and put it in a plastic bag and hid it in the bushes. The man that drove the pop truck gave them plenty of openers, so they wouldn't miss any. My mom soon caught up with us because we both had the grape pop on our upper lips from turning it up when we drank it. She spanked us both and made us stay in the house all day. So, we quit that, but my brother got another idea. He told me when the pop truck comes, he would climb up on it and get us a grape pop and I had to watch for him. He done this for about twenty times before mom caught him. He was throwing the pop in the bushes by the creek, and he got the soap from the kitchen so we could wash our lips so she couldn't see any grape pop. One day, she was watching. She gave us a hard spanking and made us stay in all day. We agreed we wouldn't do that anymore.

The man who set up the business for my dad had the outbuilding done and made a bedroom in it and people were renting it on the week-ends and sometimes through the week.

Our oldest brother Herby had been drafted to the Korean War right before we moved to the beer joint, and we weren't allowed to talk about it. We cried so much. We had always asked about him and they told us he was all right and would change the subject and take our mind off it. One day, I opened the chest of drawers, and I was standing on a chair because it was the top drawer and I had seen a lot of letters from him, and I couldn't read some of the words and my aunt came into the room and seen I had found them. I told her to ask mom if she could read some to us and she did, and mom said OK. We were happy. Every letter he wrote he said he loved us and missed us, and he wanted to come home. We started crying and mom said, "That's why we don't read the letters to you, but we write back to him every time. We haven't forgotten him!"

We didn't get much family time together with them running the business. We just went in and played with the jukebox and slot machines; that was our fun, but we weren't allowed to tell people we knew.

We didn't get to play when the night crowds came. Sometimes we hit jackpots and all the money fell out and dad would open it up and stack all the coins back in. We didn't care.

I seen some man was talking to dad and told him that he got word that the competition was very mad that we had took all their business and he told dad, "You know how they are; be careful!!"

I didn't know what they meant, so I asked mom and my aunt. "They are dangerous", mom said.

Our family had to clean the counters, sweep and mop the dance floor and wipe the slot machines with a wet towel. It was Sunday and people usually started coming in about eleven a.m. Some truck drivers came by on Sundays. They would have a beer and a snack and leave, and then come back the next Sunday.

My aunt was cleaning the room in the outbuilding and changed the bed sheets. She was happy when Sundays came because everyone was tired, and they started closing at eleven p.m. We all went to bed, and we heard someone at the door and mom said, "It's three am, who could be knocking on the door so hard?" She went to the door, and it was one of the competition brothers yelling, "Your place is on fire!". "It's the competition", mom said. She was getting everyone up and we all got out of the house. We were crying. It was a terrible inferno! Dad brought his gun out with him, and my older brother Pippy ran around to the back of the house and went in and locked the door, and they were yelling his name for him to come out. No one could get back in the front door, so dad ran around to the back door and was shooting his gun calling for our brother to come out. He was so frightened; he didn't know what to do.

We went back to the front of the house and mom and our aunt were dipping the water and throwing it on the front of the old house. It had brick siding material on it and the beer was popping through the wall blowing up, can after can, making a zing noise as it blew through the wall. Finally, they got enough water on it and the beer quit popping through the wall.

We were all scared and exhausted, and my heart was beating so fast. I had never seen a fire like that. The man who woke us up was still out by the road in a taxi. He said he was coming from somewhere and seen the building on fire and burning badly and woke us up. It was an awful sight. It was beginning to break daylight and the smoke was horrific. The frames of the coolers had collapsed to ashes. Some of the slot machines didn't melt all the way.

The business had burned down completely before the guy knocked on the door. It was a traumatic day for all of us. Mom told dad that man that was in the taxi woke us up because of the children... "Mercy" spared us! Mom told dad she wanted to take the children back to the old house; we were scared. He said, "Give me four days to straighten some things out", and she said OK.

The house was still intact except for the front where it caught fire and burnt the siding, and it turned black and had some holes in it from when the beer blew out the wall. The siding was really smelling very bad, but dad said they could fix the holes in it. Dad got a man with a truck to go get him some tools he could work with. The man came back with a pick, crowbar, two shovels and a wheelbarrow. He said he'd come back the next morning and he left. We went into the house, and we were still smelling all the ashes. The metal things were melted and smelled like rust, bad. There were chemical smells coming from all of it, too. We were happy we didn't die.

"BUILDING THE PLACE BACK"

Suddenly someone was knocking on the back door and dad got his gun and asked, "Who is it?" and the man at the door answered and dad let him in. It was the man who set the business up. He said he heard about it early in the morning and that's why he came. He told my dad, "We know who done this and we will just be quiet, and I'll build it back bigger and better, and if they do something they will be sorry!", he quietly told my dad. He didn't want to talk in front of us.

The next morning the man was back with the truck and him and dad started prying the slot machines open and they had long stacks of coins that had melted together, and dad was putting them in the wheelbarrow. They were heavy and there were some coins not stuck together but they were very black, and I asked if me and my younger brother could have them and dad said yes, but that we had to wash them with Bon Ami, a scrubbing powder. We got mom's dishpan and put water in it and used the scrub powder. The water was getting black very fast, and we kept changing it, but our hands were getting really dirty. Our older brother gave us two old socks to put the coins in and we divided them. Mom told us to come in. She was cooking food for all of us. The man and dad finally quit working on the house, and he took all his tools with him and left the wheelbarrow. He said to keep it, as it was old, and dad thanked him. So, they must have been his own tools. Mom said, "I am going to the old house tomorrow." She said she would take us, and our older brother and aunt would stay in that house because some people were supposed to come and clear all the debris and get it ready for the new place to be built.

We were feeling more content in the old house. Mom and dad took us grocery shopping and she cooked for us, and dad went to work that evening. We didn't have enough furniture at the old house, but we had two beds, a stove, a Frigidaire, a table and four chairs. Mom had our clothes on hangers and hung them in the closet, and she tore the brown grocery bags and placed them in the corner on the floor in the living room and put the towels, wash cloths and toothbrushes and toothpaste on top of the bags. We had only a few dishes and silverware in the stove oven. My brother and I wanted to go to the neighbor's house which was the distance of about two city blocks walking on the dirt driveway and my mom said we couldn't go because their mom would ask questions about the business burning down, and we weren't allowed to talk about it.

I heard mom talking to dad the next day and she said she was afraid to go back to the new business, and he said it would be ok. He said, "If I don't do that, when another strike comes, we won't have any money again. She said, "Maybe we can run it for six months and save some money and tell the man he will have to get someone else to run it." Dad said, "Let's see how things go."

My mom was tired, and my aunt was going every two weeks to see her little boy who was staying with my grandmother. My aunt was missing him.

We will all drive up to the business and see if all the debris is cleaned up in the morning, which will be Saturday, and dad will be off from work.

We all got up early and stopped at a grocery store and got some hot dogs already made and a pop to drink and headed up there. We really wanted to see our brother and our aunt. We were almost there, and I heard dad say, "Oh my God!" There were a lot of guys there working, and dad said they already poured a concrete floor and were putting up the block around it and he couldn't believe it. He told mom, "The man said he could have built back in six weeks." Our aunt and brother said they were working everyday till dark. We were there about one hour, and the man came that owned the place and had a big truck for him there, and dad asked, "What is the truck for?" He said it was for the workers to ride back home in, and he handed one of the guys the keys and told him to take all the workers home and bring them back in the morning. He bought the workers food and drinks and was good to them. He told dad, "This place will be finished in three weeks. I have plenty of workers and one more load of materials to finish this. Then the jukebox, coolers and slot machines will come, and we can open for business again." It was a strange feeling for all of us to see the place being built again. It was like something had died and was coming back again.

The workers had put something on the front of the house and covered all the black burned stuff. Everything was changing so fast it didn't seem real. We stayed the evening with my aunt and brother, then we went home again. The man went home, and the workers were still there when we went back to the old house. We were tired and mom made us some food fast and made baby brother a bottle and let me hold the bottle for him, and we all got ready for bed.

We were tired and went to sleep. We got up the next morning and mom was cooking breakfast and talking to dad telling him she was afraid something else might happen when we go back there. He told her he didn't think so. He went to work, and we sat on the porch in a swing, and she asked if we wanted to go back there, and we said yes. She asked why and my brother said we can play the jukebox and dance there and I said, "Yes, that's right." We didn't have anything to do there at the old house because she wouldn't let us talk to the neighbors. She washed a few clothes, made us some sandwiches, and bathed the baby. It was getting late, and we had to go to bed.

The next morning dad got up and got all the metal coins that had melted together and put them in different boxes. He said the banker would weigh them and give him what they are worth! When he came out of the bank mom asked how much he gave him for all that and he said about four hundred dollars. Mom said it looked like more and asked what they will do with all the melted metal. Dad said they will send it to the mint. We will go back to the place in two days. Time was going fast, and we went back up and they were carrying slot machines to the back of the building on a large truck. Then they were left on a big counter. The jukebox was on a large floor and not plugged in. There was a pop cooler at the end of the counter, also there was a back room with three pop coolers and a room beside it that had a door you went through, and it had a long table with twelve chairs. I asked mom if we would eat there, and she said, "No, that's a poker table and you will still eat in the house." My aunt and older brother were happy we came back. The man that set the place up came by and he had a big truck to stock the place with beer, snacks, pop and chips. He had two young guys with him, and he told them where to take everything. They worked for about three hours and my aunt and older brother helped them. Everything was in place. The man told dad, "You can open tomorrow." Mom didn't look happy.

We drove back to the old place and got all our clothes and things together to leave early the next morning. We got up really early and put all our things in the car, and drove back to the new place, and my aunt and older brother wiped everything down and cleaned the counters.

We were now back in school, and my aunt had to drive us again. Our teacher taught three different grades in one big room; and she stayed busy.

"TWO CHILDREN PLAYING DETECTIVES"

My brother and I were told to watch out for the two brothers (the competition) from town and to tell our family if we had seen them. My aunt drove us to school and as we got out of the car she said, "Remember what your mom said, not to tell anyone about the terrible fire. We can't let people know about that." I promised her as well as my mom that I wouldn't tell anyone about it. Dad was still working the evening shift at the mines and the business had a lot of the customers come back. It was getting crowded on Friday and Saturday, and dad was having poker games on Saturday night with some of his friends he knew and other people. The big poker table was in the back room and only certain people could go in it. My younger brother and I were not allowed to talk about it with anyone. My aunt told me, and my brother, "Don't forget to watch for the brothers from town that said your dad took all their business." We were to tell them if we saw them and not to talk to them. We promised them we would do that. We went to school every day and we asked my aunt if she would pick her son up and let him stay a weekend with us. She said yes if it wouldn't be too much on my mom with my baby brother. She asked mom, and she said yes. We couldn't wait till Friday; she would pick him up while we were at school and take him back on Sunday. Finally, Friday came, and we went to school, and when our aunt came to pick us up, she had her little boy with her, and we kept hugging him. We were all so happy. My brother took him over to the jukebox and our older brother gave him a quarter to put in the jukebox. He held him up so he could put the quarter in it and older brother punched in five different records so he could dance with him, and we were so happy, and he was, too.

After the music stopped, my younger brother wanted to show him the slot machines. Mom took some dimes from the cash register, and we went to the slot room and his mom held him up and helped him pull the handle with her help and the coins hit the jackpot! All the coins were coming out and he was scared at first, but then he liked it. Mom said to let him keep the money and double bagged it for him. Mom cooked dinner for us, and my aunt ate dinner with us kids and she went back to the business; mom and my older brother came back to the house to eat. Dad was at work, and he usually would eat it the next day. We had a good time with our little cousin. We showed him the creek and the small building, but he wanted to stay by the jukebox, and they held him up and put money in and he punched the buttons. There were a lot of Hank Williams songs on the jukebox and most people liked him, so they played that more than others. Time went by really fast, and it was Sunday morning, and our aunt had to take her son back to grandmother.

Her son didn't want to leave. We asked if we could go with her to take him back home and mom said yes. We all got ready and got in the car. We were happy because we would get to see our grandparents. We didn't get to see them often. Everyone was too busy to take us.

We finally arrived and they were happy to see us. Grandfather said we had grown a lot and that I looked just like my dad. He never really liked my dad because he drank and gambled a lot. Grandmother made us lunch because auntie told her we had to get back soon. We bid farewell to them and headed home. We finally arrived home and there were several cars at the business, and we went through the front of the business and the jukebox was playing and some people were dancing and the rest of them were drinking and playing the slot machines. Mom was in the house cooking dinner for everyone. She told us to take a bath because we had to go to school in the morning, so we did that and laid our school clothes out for the morning. We never got to eat with all of us together because someone had to stay in the place.

My aunt got ready and drove us to school the next morning and reminded us not to talk about the business or the fire. I told her she didn't have to tell me anymore; I wouldn't forget. Our younger brother mostly talked about playing marbles and baseball at school. The teacher kept all of us busy and sometimes she let us sing songs while she graded papers. Another day went by, and my aunt was picking us up to go home. My brother and I were talking as she drove home, and we told her we missed the old house and getting to go to town. She said she did, too.

"GAMBLING TABLE WAS FULL ON WEEKENDS"

The business was doing well on Friday and Saturday. They didn't have enough room for parking and cars were parked all up and down the road. Dad was running the poker table on Friday and Saturday night, and he quit locking the doors and younger brother and I kept walking through the doors looking at the men playing cards. Dad said we could walk through if we didn't make any noise or run, so we kept it up and did what he said, because we liked seeing all the money on the table.

Mom was growing tired having to take care of baby brother and work in the place, too. Time was passing fast, and baby brother was growing a lot, but still had to have a lot of attention. School would be out in about three weeks and our aunt would have more time not having to drive us every day, there and back.

We asked dad if he would take us to see his sister so we could see the brother he let go to stay with her. He said he would take a vacation and take us there. We were happy to hear that. School was finally out, and dad had a three-week vacation, and the third week was supposed to be our week to go see his sister. During the first week, the competition from where we used to live showed up and asked if he could play poker with dad on Friday with the others. This was the guy that woke us up when the other place was burning up. Dad told him no, and that there were too many people playing. He quoted to dad, "You have those games on Friday and Saturday, right?" Dad answered, "Sometimes."

He stayed a while and was playing slot machines in the back room, then left. My mom, aunt and older brother were scared and told dad we have to be careful; he is up to something. The games went on that weekend. A strange man came in late Monday afternoon, and he gave me and my brother money for the jukebox and we played music he told us to. He was at the counter telling dad he knows one of his friends and called him by name and my dad said you know him by name, you know a good man. He told dad his friend said dad was having a poker game Friday and Saturday at four pm and asked if he could come; dad said yes. My aunt was listening to that conversation, and she asked why dad said he could come to the poker game. Dad said, "He is ok and knows my friend, and he was nice to the kids." My aunt told mom about the conversation, and she said dad shouldn't have done that. My older brother told me and younger brother to watch for him and if he comes back to tell him if we see him.

"DAD ARRESTED"

My younger brother and I watched for him every day. Finally, he came on Saturday at about three pm. He had another man with him and said he wanted to play the slots, so the one man went back to play the slots and the other man continued to talk to dad and followed dad back to the poker room with seven other men. My younger brother and I went out the back door and came in the front door and my aunt motioned to me and I walked over to her, and she whispered in my ear for me to go back in the slot room and watch the man in the slot room that came in with the one that went to the poker room with dad. About ten minutes later he left the slot room and walked around to the back door of the poker room and my aunt told my older brother somethings up and my younger brother was still in the poker room and mom was in the house with baby brother. So,

I ran back out the front door around to the back and seen the man going in the poker room and followed him in. Once he was in, the man that brought him in jumped up from the table and they both pulled guns and said, "Everybody up against the wall. You are under arrest!" My younger brother and I were screaming, "Don't hurt my daddy!" The one that was playing poker told the other one to get these kids out of here! My brother was kicking him, and he put his gun in his pocket and picked my brother up and held him under his arm and my brother was pinching him and trying to bite him saying, "Don't kill my daddy." I was saying, "Please God, don't let him kill my daddy!" Then he grabbed me by the hand and was pulling me out the back door and my brother still under his arm kicking and screaming. I will never forget my dad's face. He was so scared and white. They were all up against the wall with their arms up.

Mom went to the front and told all the customers, "It's a raid.", and they were getting in their cars and leaving. Suddenly, a large bus pulled up and all the men from the poker table were being handcuffed and put in the bus. The man that was holding us let my mom have us and she was crying, too. Also, two big trucks loaded all the slot machines up and the poker table, the chairs, jukebox, and 1900 cases of beer. They took everything. My aunt told them we don't have a way to make a living, leave us some beer and one slot machine, and they left ten cases of beer. Mom wanted to make us something to eat, but we were too upset to eat, so we all went to bed. Mom said we would have to go to the jail in the morning and see if we can get dad out of jail. The next day was Sunday. Mom said it might be difficult.

"SUNDAY A.M."

Someone was knocking on our door at seven a.m. It was the man who set dad up in business. He told mom not to worry. He knew the judge and if there was a jury, he would know all of them, so there won't be any problems. Mom told him they took all the money and he said, "Don't worry about it. I'll go with all of you on Monday. Meet me by the county jail." Mom said OK.

We all met the man there Monday morning and they took my dad to the courthouse, and set a bond for him, and the man paid them.

"TRIAL"

The man set a trial date with a jury and the man convinced us all that everything would be all right. The man had been collecting money from dad all along, every two months, my dad called it rent money. I never knew what he paid. We departed and the man told us bye and handed dad an envelope and said he would come back and see him next Friday to talk and I asked dad if he gave them money and he said, "You don't need to know everything and don't tell anyone about this." I said, "OK."

We were still shaken by this. It was like a horrible dream. Mom told dad she couldn't take any more of this; she was tired and nervous. My aunt and older brother weren't anxious to do this again. My younger brother and I wanted to go back to the old house where we could ride the school bus again and see our friends. We knew we would miss the jukebox and entertaining the people. They would throw quarters, dimes, and half dollar coins on the floor, and we would pick them up when we quit dancing and go play the slots. They were good people; never had any fights, nothing bad happened. Dad was a very friendly person, and he was liked by everyone.

My mom was the kindest person to everyone. Dad upset her with the way he wanted to live and that made her angry with him. Today is Friday, and the man is supposed to come by to talk to my dad. We all got up early and we quickly ate breakfast, and we heard a knock on the door. It was the man. He sat down with dad. Mom told us to go into the living room and be quiet. Mom asked the man if he wanted a cup of coffee, and he said yes. My older brother got baby brother his bottle of milk and he was quiet. We were trying to listen to what the man was saying to dad. He said, "Let's hold off for about three months. We will have to see how things go at the court, also." The man said everything will be fine. Dad told him, "We are moving back to the old house temporarily, and I will check this place weekly", and he said OK. He told dad, "I will be going to court with you, and you don't have anything to worry about." He also said he would come to our old house every other Saturday and talk with dad. Dad said OK, and the man said bye. I asked dad if he would take us to see his sister as he promised, and he said yes. She lived in another state and she's the one that took our brother that dad says doesn't belong to him; but we all loved him. Dad asked mom to get him his wallet out of a box she kept it in at the house behind the business and let him count the vacation money he got from work. He said we had nine hundred dollars, and we would leave on a Friday and come back on a Friday. We had enough money.

My aunt went to my grandmothers for two days. She took her little boy to town and bought my brother and me some new clothes for vacation and school. We were happy mom and dad had been paying her while she worked at the business and mom told her she shouldn't be spending money on us, but she said that's what she wanted to do. We will be starting back school after vacation, and dad will be going back to work.

Time seemed to be passing fast and we would be leaving early Friday to go see our aunt, dad's sister. We all got our clothes ready Thursday and got up really early Friday morning and left. Dad stopped to get gas and we all got a hot dog and a pop, and he kept driving all day and we finally got there at five pm and our aunt had cooked dinner for all of us. Our brother had gained weight and looked so good. He got healthy, having food to eat (no strikes). Our aunt had her TV on, and it was the first one I ever saw. My younger brother and I were touching the screen with our fingers and mom walked in and said, "That's not real and don't touch it!" So, we left it alone. My uncle told us he would take us to an amusement park tomorrow and we were happy to hear that, and we went to bed thinking about it. We got up early the next morning and we were glad everything was so peaceful. My older brother, uncle and dad went to watch the news on TV, and we thanked them for everything! They watched TV, and mom and both of my aunts took me and my younger baby brother to the kitchen and sat us at the table. Our aunt took a roast she had cooked the night before and some boiled potatoes from the oven. She had made a large salad before we got up this morning and put everything on the table. They called dad, our brother, and our uncle into eat, and she told us the best is yet to come!

We all hurriedly ate, waiting for the best; our meal was fantastic, and our aunt cleared the table and wiped it. She went to the refrigerator and pulled out two large cheesecakes and cut them, and mom got the dessert plates and forks, and our aunt got a big bowl of fresh strawberries from the Frigidaire and placed them on the cheesecakes, and they looked delicious! Dad's sister had an old highchair and she put baby brother in it so mom could help him eat. The cheesecakes and strawberries were delicious. My aunt took the cheesecakes and strawberries to the living room for dad, son and my uncle where they were watching the news and they said they loved them!

My aunt told mom to let us all get in the showers tonight and mom grouped us together and had us divided, and I bathed youngest brother for the first time. We all liked the showers. We mostly had to bathe in wash tubs at home. My aunt had both tubs and toilets in her house; what a convenience! She knew we didn't live as well as her.

We all got up a little later the next morning. Dad told mom it was on the news that his mines were going on strike and that worried her. His sister begged him to stay but he was worried about his job! His sister gave us cookies she had baked. We really liked them. We thanked them for everything, and we hugged them. We were all happy; it was so good to get away from bad things that had happened to us. My Aunt Edith told my mom if dad was on strike again, she would find someone who needed domestic help and have a job and our older brother said he would find a job. Somehow, we all looked out for each other more than we had before. I think we appreciated life more and was happy none of us died through all the bad things. My younger brothers and the baby had fallen asleep, and I was extremely tired. My aunt told me to lay my head on a pillow in her lap and I did, and the next thing I heard was, "We will be home in two hours! So, we must find a restaurant to eat at before dark." We were all tired from traveling.

We continued driving and dad saw a small restaurant ahead with red and green lights on the front of it and he stopped, and we all went in. The waitress seated us in a booth and got a highchair for baby brother. The waitress gave us the menu that was one large sheet of paper that had just a dinner menu that's served after four pm. We could have a cheeseburger or a steak and French fries or regular fried potatoes, so we all chose the cheeseburger and French fries, and they were really good. It was a very small restaurant and the waitress, and the owners were really nice. We ate very quickly and headed for home; we were all very tired. The kids fell asleep once we were back on the road. Dad said we would be home in forty minutes, and mom said she hoped so. Our aunt was really tired. She was yawning a lot. Finally, we turned off on the road near our house and ten minutes later we were on the dirt road to our house. I was so happy! Dad pulled us close as he could get to the house so we could get out easily and we did it in a hurry.

We were all getting our pajamas on and going to bed. Dad didn't turn the news on, as he was so tired.

"NEXT DAY"

Dad got up early and said he will have to go to town today to see if they are talking about a strike, so we will stay home and hear what he has to say when he comes home. Our neighbors were greeting us at the school bus stop where they would pick us up and take us to school. We were happy to see them. It seemed like a long day at school. Our teacher had to organize three grades in one room. Another teacher had two higher grades in another big room. They worked hard and they cared. The teacher in the big room had the big bell in the ceiling and she pulled the rope to ring the bell for lunch time and later for going home. It was an old school with outside toilets. Some of the kids lived near the school and went home for lunch.

Most of the people were poor in the Appalachians. They all traded chicken for pork or beef, and some had cows and sold milk and butter, and many had nothing. They tried to help each other. Some of the miners had Black Lung and they could hardly breathe from breathing the coal dust. It was sad for them…. They had to quit work.

Dad came home and told mom the union said they would be picketing, and they would tell them what day to walk out on strike this week, and mom looked very sad; and all the family knew what this meant. We had been through it many times. My aunt and older brother said we will make it, don't worry.

We got through Thursday, and we thought everything was OK. My younger brother and I came home from school and mom and aunt were cooking dinner and older brother was chopping wood for the cook stove and mom said that older brother was quitting school. He told her he was old enough and he didn't want to go anymore. She begged him to go but he said no. She said your dad will handle this. Dad was late coming home and mom said they must have walked out on strike, so we will eat now and put food away for him. Finally, dad arrived three hours late and said the day shift had walked off and the union had them wait until the afternoon shift arrived so they could take their place picketing. We all felt bad hearing this.

We found ourselves in the same situation as we had many times before and most people weren't prepared for it. My brother and I continued going to school and my older brother was getting jobs in town doing different things for people.

"KIDS SHARING LUNCH!"

Our aunt got a job with an elderly man delivering milk and eggs to peoples' doors. My aunt and brother gave mom money for groceries. We were barely making it. Finally, dad was getting strike fund money weekly; it was only a few dollars. My brother and I had crackers with peanut butter between them. We had to go behind the school and the teacher gave us cups and we pumped water from the school ground pump to drink. We were thirsty eating peanut butter and crackers. Some of the other kids had white bread with marshmallow cream, peanut butter and sliced bananas between the white bread. Many of the kids shared their sandwiches with us and we appreciated it, although we were embarrassed about it. Most of the kids had a lunch bucket and a thermos bottle for their drink. We had only a brown paper bag. The teacher started buying small cartons of milk again and setting them on a table and said whoever wants milk to come get it. We were embarrassed but we drank it. Everyone was well behaved.

We were happy to be back in the old house, even though we didn't have much money. There was a beer joint below our house on the road. It had come to have big crowds of people at night. The man who ran it said he was going to rent it out next summer and move to Tennessee with his family. My brother and I sold him pop bottles that we picked up on the road and we got enough money to go to the movies. The man had an addition on the place, it had five motel rooms he rented to people, and we sometimes talked to customers. There was a couple (man and wife) who had come back from Florida, and they had some huge oranges. They looked like grapefruits, they were so big, and they gave us each one and we ate it so fast. We were really hungry. I heard the woman whisper to him, "They are hungry, let's give them some more", and they gave us four to take home. We hurried home and showed our mother, and she couldn't believe how big they were. Mom ate half of one and saved some for the rest of the family. Mom and dad went to the post office once a week to get the mail and they came home with two big packages, and they were really heavy. They were from two paratroopers we all knew and loved, and they loved us. They each mailed a parachute to mom so she could make us blouses and shirts. One was white with little white checks in it, and the other was bright orange with small checks.

"CHECKING THE PARACHUTES"

My brother and I were trying to pick them up and we couldn't; they were so heavy. Mom said she would make me some blouses and my brother some shirts out of them. I told her I loved the orange one, and to make me an orange one first, and she said OK. She could sew very good on her machine, and she got to work right away and made me the orange blouse. I wore it to school Monday morning and my teacher called my name and said, "Where did you get that pretty blouse?" I said, "It's a parachute." She said, "A what?" I repeated it and she called me up to her desk and said she didn't understand what I said, and I told her some paratroopers sent two parachutes to mom and that we all knew them, and they sent them so mom could make us some clothes with the material. The teacher said, "It's very pretty." I said, "She is making me a white one, too." She said, "No one will have pretty blouses like you." I was a little embarrassed and when I got on the school bus the kids were talking about it, but they were being very nice and asked me how mom made it, and I said with a sewing machine. I couldn't wait to get home and tell mom how the teacher liked my blouse. She asked, "Did you tell her it was a parachute that it was made from?" I said, "Yes." She said, "You should not have said that." I told her she didn't tell me not to; and she said she forgot, and for me not to tell anyone else. I said, "I won't."

We were hoping for the strike to end but dad said it may be a long time, and that we must wait and see. It was Monday, and we had just got off the school bus and my dad had come home from picketing for the union, and someone was knocking on our door. I opened it and a man I didn't know asked for dad. My mom and I ran to get my dad and he came to the door and the man quickly handed him some papers. Mom and dad sat down and started looking at them and said they were court papers for his trial next week, and it is on a Thursday. Mom said we will have to take the kids out of school. Dad said he wouldn't be with the strikers that day. He said he will have to tell them he was sick!

Dad didn't want them to know he had to go to court. I asked mom, "Does he have to go to the jail?" She said, "We hope not." She told me not to tell this to anyone and I said OK. My brother and aunt came home from their jobs and mom told them the court date was set and they all seemed worried. Mom had dinner cooked and we were all at the table. I asked dad, "If you go to jail, what will we do?" Mom said, "We are not going to talk about that." After we got through eating, she told me and my younger brother we could go outside and play for an hour. I think they all wanted to talk and not let us know what they were saying about the court. Mom called us in and told us we had to have a bath and lay all our school clothes out for tomorrow. Then we did a little homework we had from school and went to bed.

It was early morning again and mom was cooking. It seemed like it was earlier than usual and I asked her. She said it was twenty minutes earlier and I asked her why, and she said she didn't sleep well. My brother and I ate and started getting ready to catch the school bus. Mom told me not to tell anyone about the court and I promised I wouldn't. My dad got up to go with the strikers, and my aunt and older brother got up to go to their jobs. It seemed like a long day after hearing mom up early. I think she is worried.

We were happy to see our friends at school. Every one of us was nice to each other. It seemed like time went fast after lunch. The bell was ringing, and the bus was waiting for us to come out. We all quickly boarded, and we were all talking quietly to each other on the bus. We weren't allowed to make a lot of noise. We had to be respectable, and we were. We were soon at our bus stop, and we quickly got off and went home. Dad came home about a half an hour after us, and then my brother and our aunt came. We all sat down for dinner that mom had made, then there was a knock on the door. Dad said he would get it, and it was the man who owned the business, and he had another man with him and said this is your lawyer and dad shook hands with him. Mom offered them to eat but they said they had already eaten. They told dad to quickly finish his dinner and he did and went to the living room with them to talk. My mom and aunt quickly cleaned the kitchen up. The lawyer told my mom, older brother and aunt to sit up close with them on the day of court. He told mom to hold the baby in the court room and we all said we would do what he said.

"COURT DAY"

Time passed very quickly, and it was Thursday morning, and mom was waking us up early. She had coffee made for them and doughnuts, and we had cereal with bananas cut up in it. We were eating and no one was talking much. Mom told us to brush our teeth and wash our face and hands. My aunt helped us get dressed fast. Dad told us all to hurry up that he had to be in the court room at ten a.m., and he had to see the attorney and the man who owned the business at eight thirty a.m. in a small restaurant near the courthouse. We had to drive back to the town where the business was and then into the town where the courthouse was. Dad parked the car about three buildings down from the restaurant, and we walked to it. We all went in, and dad ordered all of them a coffee and me and my brother a hot chocolate. Dad said when the man comes in, we all were to go to the car and my aunt would take the baby; and him and mom would stay at the restaurant talking to the attorney and the man. My younger brother and I had just finished our hot chocolate and the man, and the attorney walked in, and dad told our aunt to take us to the car. I didn't want to leave dad with them. Dad was dressed up in a black pinstriped suit, white shirt and a tie, and we all had our best clothes on that morning. Dad's face looked like the day those men came in with the guns on them. He was very white. My aunt and older brother got us back in the car and we were all scared. It seemed like a long time before dad and mom came back to the car, but my aunt said it was less than an hour. Dad said we would go to the courthouse, and we could use the bathrooms before we went to the courtroom. Mom told us to be quiet or we would be in trouble. The courthouse was a big building, one of the biggest ones we had seen since we left Baltimore. There were a lot of people in the courtroom and some policemen. The man and the attorney came in and was talking to dad and the attorney moved up front with dad and everyone got really quiet. The judge walked in, and a lot of people came in and filled seats across from the judge. The judge called dad's name, and the attorney walked up with dad and the judge asked my dad to face all those people who filled those chairs across from him. The attorney was talking to them and having dad answer some questions, and I couldn't understand what they were saying. The judge finally asked the seated people to go to a room to reach a verdict and the people went out and the judge recessed the court for half an hour and said everyone is to come back in one half hour. We all walked out, and the attorney and the man were laughing, and I heard dad say, "I don't know." We all proceeded back into the court room, and the judge sent someone to the jury room, and they said they couldn't reach a verdict, so he gave them fifteen more minutes and they said it was a hung jury. I didn't know what that meant. The attorney was whispering to the judge and the court was over, and people started leaving the court room. The attorney, the man, and dad walked over to us and said we could go home, and my older brother was looking to the back of the court room and whispering to my aunt and mom said, "What's wrong?" My aunt said my older brother had her to look back and she seen the brother of the competition who had woken us up when the other place burned down and my aunt said, "The dirty son of a bitch came to the court to see if he would be put in prison. When he seen us looking back, he left the court room."

I heard the attorney tell dad, "That man (meaning the man who owned the business) runs this whole county." I asked dad if he told the attorney they took the cash register full of his money and he said, "Shut up", and the attorney laughed, and we departed. When we got in the car I asked, "What does that man run in the county?" He said, "Nothing, and don't say anything about that again." I said OK.

"SELLING POP BOTTLES TO GO SEE TIM HOLT, THE COWBOY MOVIE STAR"

We were happy to go home together, and dad would have to get up early to picket because he missed a day of it and had to tell the head man of the union, he was sick. We got up and went to school. I was smiling at my teacher, and she asked if we were sick the day before, and mom said to tell her we went to see our grandparents that they were sick, and she said she hoped they got well. It was Friday and my younger brother, and I had plans to pick up pop bottles to sell so we could go to the movies. Mom made dinner early and we went down to the road and went into the weeds along the highway where people in cars threw their pop bottles out. Some of the weeds were really high but we found a lot of bottles in them. My brother had a cloth sack to put the bottles in. He kept it under the porch where we could always find it. My brother found out from the boys at school that his favorite, Cowboy Tim Holt, was coming to our movie theater, and he really wanted to see him in person. There was also another guy that was a big star, and his name was Lash Larue, a whip-cracking Indian and my brother liked both, and I did too. My brother counted our pop bottles, and we had twenty-four, so we took them to the grocery store, and he gave us fifty cents so we each had twenty-five cents. We got a surprise when we got in line to see Tim Holt. We had to pay twenty-five cents each to see him, so we didn't care about the popcorn. We were very excited to see movie stars in person.

Music began to play, and Lash Larue came out cracking his whip and wore a vest with rhinestones and Indian markings on it with fringe on the sides of his pants and rhinestones. He did a lot of tricks with everyone cheering him on. He was on stage about thirty minutes and said, "Now I am going to introduce the star of the show, Mr. Tim Holt." Everyone was screaming and music was still playing. Tim Holt was circled with Lash Larue's whip, and he was jumping over it, and they turned the music down some and Tim Holt began talking to the audience and then yodeling. Everyone was screaming happy and enjoying the show.

They stayed on stage for about an hour together and then said we will pick some people to come backstage with us and get acquainted. We were in the front row and my little brother was so happy. He was saying, "Pick me!" He picked both of us and several other people in different rows. He picked twelve people total to come and get acquainted. Ushers took us behind the curtains and others followed us up. Tim Holt and his wife were sitting in chairs, and they had other chairs for guests. My little brother held his hand up and said, "I want to ask you a question." Tim Holt told him to come up to him and he sat my brother on his lap and said, "What do you want to ask me?" My little brother started talking like a man to him and asked if he could go home with him, and Tim Holt said I don't think your mother would let you; and my brother said ask my sister and pointed to me. I was afraid to say no and I said yes, and my brother said, "I know she will let me because I love you." All the people were laughing at him, and I didn't know he was going to ask that.

Tim Holt was having a hard time talking him out of it. He told him, "Bring your mom here tomorrow and I will talk to her and if she says yes, I will take you." My brother asked where they would meet him, and he said in front of the theater at twelve o'clock noon. I had no idea he would say that. All the adults were still laughing at him. My brother said, "Let's go outside and maybe dad will be here to pick us up and I can get him to come in."

Our dad was waiting for us, and my brother started telling him Tim Holt will take me to Hollywood if mom tells him I can go tomorrow. Dad told him he is joking with you. My brother said he was not. Dad told him to wait until he asked his mother. My brother got up really early and began telling mom what Tim Holt said and she told him he was just joking, and he knows we would not let you go with a stranger. My brother was getting mad over this so mom said let's talk about something else. He said, "I don't want to.", and started crying. He cried for about an hour and dad told him he would take him to town, and we would walk with him. He said OK but he wasn't happy.

"WANTING OUT OF THE MOUNTAINS"

We got up early and asked if we could eat cereal for breakfast and mom said OK, but we had to drink an extra cup of milk.

Our dad didn't have to be with the strikers today, so he drove us to town. We asked him if he would let us stay in town for two hours and he said, "How will you know when two hours are up?" I said, "The big clock outside the jewelry store, or we can ask people." He said, "OK, where do you want me to pick you up?" We said the drug store. He said OK and pulled out to go back home. We felt so free being in town, getting to see all the people we know, and talking to them. I had to be careful and not say anything my parents told me not to say. When we stopped on the corner of the street, I would look up in the sky at the planes wishing that I was on one of them. The mountains were so high the planes looked very small, and I didn't care where they were going, I just wanted out of there. We were really getting tired, and we just passed the jewelry store, and we had fifteen minutes to get to the drug store. When we rounded the corner, we saw dad's car and my brother wanted to get in the back seat, so I got in the front. Dad asked if we liked all the walking and I said yes, but my brother was snoring. He fell asleep fast. Soon we were pulling up to the house and my brother woke up.

"BROTHER COMING HOME FROM KOREA"

We told our dad we wanted to go to the movies more often and we could walk around. He said maybe. The weather was getting much cooler, and he was worried that the strike would last through Christmas. My aunt and my brother were still working their little jobs, and my aunt was still going to see her little boy at my grandmother's, and she came back every Sunday evening after spending the day with him. My older brother didn't work on Sunday, and he sometimes went to the movies with another boy who was his friend and none of us had to walk to town. Someone always gave us a ride to and from town. We all knew each other, and we were all kind to each other. My dad went to the post office on Monday and our oldest brother had written a letter. He was coming home from the Korean War the next week. We couldn't wait to see him. Our baby brother was running all over the house and making all of us laugh. He was getting bigger, and he was very funny. It's very cold outside and the weeds had died. We could see the pop bottles better, so my brother said let's go get some pop bottles and we went out to get them. We had about twenty and we took them to the man below us who bought them sometimes and he told us he will be renting the place to a colored man who will still serve beer, liquor and food, and we asked if he would buy pop bottles and he said he was sure he would, and that made us happy. We earned our movie money with the pop bottles, and we didn't have to ask dad for it. We ran home to tell dad that the man is going to rent the place and he told us he had already told him that.

It's Friday and my aunt and my mom went out to get some groceries. They were planning on having a big dinner for our oldest brother who was coming home tomorrow. They came home and made hot dogs and chili for us, and my aunt made a big cake and fried up a lot of chicken for tomorrow when our brother arrives. We were anxious to see him. We all got up early Saturday knowing that our brother would arrive. Mom made breakfast for us, and our aunt was making coleslaw and icing the cake. She cooked green beans and corn and made some baked potatoes. She worked really hard. Mom said our brother will be flown in and then they will take him to the nearest bus station, and they will bring him to the road below our house. He is supposed to arrive at one pm., and we were anxiously waiting for him. My aunt had bought some crepe paper in different colors and cut it in long pieces and taped it to the ceiling in the kitchen and made long streamers in different colors and she taped the bottom of them to the back of our chairs at the table; it looked really pretty, and she made crepe paper flowers and put one beside each plate.

It was a few minutes before one o'clock and we were all excited. Dad said the bus was late because they had to drop other soldiers off and it took time. We were all sitting in the living room looking out the front door for him and we heard the back door open, and we ran to the kitchen, and it was him! We were all hugging him, and we were happy he never died, and he kept hugging us. It was so good he came home. We were afraid he would get killed, but God brought him home to us!

My aunt told us to all go into the living room and she would prepare the table for us to eat. She made everything look so good. We were all eating and looking at him. He looked really good, and it was a great day in our life. We all finished eating and he got his duffle bag and brought it into the living room and opened it. He gave me a little doll and I thanked him. He gave mom and dad a picture album with him in different parts of Korea, and gave my aunt a necklace, and gave all three of our brothers a little knife with funny pictures on the handles, of funny faces. Mom put my baby brother's knife up. She said he is too small to play with it. Our oldest brother was still dressed like a soldier, and he said he would have to buy him some clothes when we could get to town. He thanked my aunt for the great meal she cooked. He said it was the best he had had in a long time. He told us he couldn't stay with us because he didn't want to work in the coal mines, and in a few days, he would leave and go to a northern state where his birth mother lives and get a job, and we can come see him, and he'll come see us. We all stayed up a little late talking to him, and mom told us to go to bed and we did. She said we could get up early in the morning, but we didn't, everyone was tired. They stayed up late talking. I heard someone in the kitchen, and I got up and seen mom peeling potatoes and my aunt making biscuits. They told me to be quiet and I could stay up. My aunt said it was nine o'clock, and they were trying to get breakfast done before everyone got up. My soldier brother got up and they gave him a cup of coffee and he went to the living room and sat down with it. Finally, everyone was up and washing their hands, and we all sat down for breakfast. Dad asked my brother when he had to leave and he said Tuesday morning, so we didn't have a lot of time to talk with him. He told us when I get a job, I will buy a new car and the first trip I make will be back to see all of you, and that made us happy. My aunt and mom were cleaning the kitchen up and someone was knocking on the door. My dad went to the door, and it was the man who owned the business, and dad introduced my eldest brother to him and he said my eldest brother could have a job helping my dad in a couple of months when they open up again, and my brother told him he would be going north for a job and he couldn't do that. The man told dad the strike could last a long time and you need money. Dad said he'd have to think about it. My mom didn't look happy. Finally, the man left, and my eldest brother told dad, "Don't go back to run that place for him, you know what happened the first time. Please don't take the kids back. The guys who burned the other place will do something else…. You know how they are." Dad said, "I don't think I will go back."

"TUESDAY MORNING"

My brother had everything together to leave and dad was going to drive him to the bus station with me and my brother started crying. We wanted to go to the bus station and dad said, "No, you won't stop crying." So, dad and our brother went to the car and my younger brother crawled under the bed and was screaming, and I was still crying, and I asked if we could stay home from school. Mom said we couldn't go to school crying, so we stayed home. Dad didn't get back from the bus station for a long time. He said the bus was late. Mom had to pull the bed away from the wall. My younger brother had cried himself to sleep. Mom picked him up and laid him on the bed, and he stayed asleep. My aunt and older brother had already left for their jobs. Dad told mom, "I have to find something to do. It's cold weather now and I don't have a place to find a job. Maybe I should go back to the business." Mom said, "I will not go." My baby brother was growing fast, and he was a good little boy. Dad said Christmas is coming soon and we need money. My aunt and my brother came home, and my younger brother had been awake for some time but stayed lying on the bed. He was tired from crying so much. Dad told mom he was going to town to talk to someone. Mom said, "Don't be gone too long. We have to cook." He said OK and came back in about an hour with two men with him. One of them was the man that was talking with him when he picked us up from the movies, and the other one I had seen in town, but didn't know him. My dad told my aunt and older brother to take us in the kitchen and him and my mom went in the living room with the two men. I heard them talking about beer and liquor, and they went back outside and were taking boxes out of dad's car and taking them in mom and dad's bedroom. We had two beds in the other bedroom. The men left very quickly, and my aunt set the table and mom came in and brought our dinner to the table. We all sat down to eat. My aunt asked dad, "Wasn't that dark haired man the sheriff?" Dad said yes. My aunt said, "And the other was the constable, I know him." Dad said, "Don't be talking to them. Let's talk about something else." We ate our dinner and mom told us to get in the bathtub, which was a number two wash tub. She helped me get out fast and added more water to it, and quickly bathed my younger brother. Dad and older brother went outside. It was getting dark, and they got wood and coal, and brought it in for the stove and fireplace. Mom said dad would be off strike day tomorrow, and they would go to the grocery store, and I asked, "Where did you get the money?" She said, "From heaven." Dad told me to keep my mouth shut and I said OK. Mom said when we get off the school bus tomorrow, they may not be home, but our aunt and brother would be there within half an hour. She never locked our doors. We just closed them, unless we were going on a trip, then they would lock them with a big key. My aunt put me and my brother to bed and they stayed up talking.

The next morning, I heard dad getting up early before anyone else got up, which was unusual. He had to be at a union meeting with the strikers and he had to leave early, so he was making coffee. Then, I heard mom get up and she made him a sandwich to take with him and I got up when he was leaving.

"HAPPY TO TALK WITH FRIENDS"

Mom looked tired and she told me to be quiet, so I wouldn't wake everyone up. She continued quietly making breakfast and everyone was getting up, except my baby brother. My younger brother got ready for school. We hurried up so we could get to the bus stop early and talk with our neighbor friends. The weather was really cold, but we liked it, as we were talking with our friends. They asked if we had to go away anymore, and we said no, and they were happy. The school bus finally arrived, and we all got on the bus and sat down with each other. They were like family. We had known them for a long time. We were soon getting off the bus and hurrying in, hoping the teacher would let one of us ring the bell, but someone had already asked, so we all took our seats. It would soon be Christmas and all of us were asking what we were getting, and I told them I didn't know. Most of the miners were on strike but the smaller mines weren't, so almost half of the miners were still working. The day went fast, and the bell was ringing for us to go home. We walked out to the bus and the driver said we could sing Christmas songs if we wanted to.

"KEEPING BEER AND WHISKEY AGAIN"

We sang, Here Comes Santa Claus, and had just finished it and we were getting off the bus. We hurried up the dirt road and we seen our dad's car wasn't in the yard and we went in as mom had us to do. I ran into mom and dad's room and started looking for all the boxes they carried in yesterday. They had stacked them under the two beds, in the closet, and in one corner. It was all beer and one case of liquor, with the beer in the corner covered with a blanket. Our aunt and brother came in from their work, and I asked my aunt if they were going to sell beer from the house. She laughed and said, "No!" My mom and dad came home, and they had a lot of groceries, and we knew we could have something different. My aunt and mom were making chili and hot dogs for dinner. We were happy. They bought us some Kool Aid, and we liked it. After we finished, I asked mom to come to her bedroom with me and I asked, "What are we doing with the beer and whiskey?" She said, "I guess you're old enough to keep a secret." I said yes, and she said, "The two men that came to the house asked us to keep the beer and whiskey for them." She told me not to tell anyone, and I said OK.

Those men must have given my mom and dad money because we

didn't have it before. Dad had to go picket today. My aunt and brother didn't have to work today. My aunt went to see her little boy and older brother had to chop wood and stack it up, and mom had to wash everyone's clothes. It seemed like a long day. We had a little snow, so mom had me and younger brother entertaining our baby brother so she could get her work done. My aunt came back from my grandmother's, and it was getting late. Mom was cooking and she said my dad was coming home. Mom told us all to wash our hands and come to the table. We heard the door open, and it was dad. He said the union had come and talked to all the miners and had offered a raise for them and they would vote on it Monday. He seemed happy, and we were too. Mom said, "I hope they settle it before Christmas." My aunt had been getting letters from her husband in prison, and he said he was getting paroled in January, and they could go back to Baltimore, and he said he would be good. Mom said, "I hope you can believe him." Dad turned the radio on for the news, and they were saying the strike may be over next week. We all were tired and getting ready for bed and went to sleep.

"MONDAY MORNING"

We were all filled with hope, and we were all talking, and we ate breakfast quickly. My aunt said she would drive us into town, and we all got ready, and she drove us to a grocery store and bought us a carton of ice cream and some cones and she drove us back home and made us some ice cream cones. We hadn't had that in a long time. We all loved it. I really didn't understand how instrumental my aunt was in our lives until we got older. She was always there for us. Mom said she would make dinner for us. She had a big kettle of pinto beans left over in the refrigerator and she quickly made cornbread and fried potatoes and we had milk. That's what we ate most of the time, though, we didn't have milk. We were anxious to see what tomorrow would hold for us, and we all got ready for bed a little early, and mom set the alarm clock, and we went to bed. Mom and dad got up early Monday morning before the rest of us and I heard them talking. Mom said, "What if you don't get back to work soon?" Dad said, "We will have to go somewhere I can get a job." Mom said, "Where would that be?" He said, "I don't know." I heard my aunt getting up, so I got up, too. My mom said I was up too early, and I would be tired at school. My dad started getting ready to go meet with the strikers and the union and I got ready for school early. My older brother and the younger brother got up and said they heard us talking. My aunt told my mom to sit down, and she made us some pancakes and syrup and we ate them. My aunt went to work to deliver the milk and eggs for the older gentleman and my older brother didn't have a job for today, so he said he would chop more wood and stack it up for the winter. My dad left to meet with the union, and soon after my younger brother and I walked to the bus stop.

We were anxious to hear what my dad would come home and tell us about his work. When we got seated at school, the teacher was talking about the mines and she said, "I hope all of your fathers get back to work." We were clapping and she smiled. The day couldn't pass fast enough; we all wanted good news. The teacher asked if I wanted to ring the bell for lunch, and I said yes. She got me a chair to climb on because I couldn't reach the rope, and when I pulled, it took me back up and then down when it rang; and the teacher would lift me off the chair. We all ran out to the little rock wall at the front of the yard and some of us sat on the rock wall to eat, but it was cold, and we sat our lunches on it and were all talking. We all had hope that our dads would be back to work. We finished our lunches and started back to the school building because we were cold. We all gathered around the big wood stove at the center of the room to warm up and the teacher told us we could take our seats after about ten minutes. The teacher said, "Let's all bow our heads and I'll say a prayer for your fathers to get back to work." It was a short day; time passed so fast, and the bell was ringing for the end of the day. We all got out the door fast and ran to the bus. Our bus driver was whistling and happy himself. We were at the second stop, and we quickly got off the bus and ran home, but our dad wasn't there yet, and my aunt still wasn't home. My mom and older brother had the table set and she was cooking. My younger brother seen a car coming to the house, but it wasn't my dad or aunt. It was one of the men that brought the whiskey to the house. My mom went to the door, and he wanted four cases of beer. My older brother loaded his car trunk with it, and he said thank you and left. My younger brother kept looking out and he said my aunt was coming home now. My aunt came in and said they had a lot of deliveries, and she was a little late.

"GOING BACK TO WORK!"

My mom told us to wash our hands and come to the table, and we all did. We sat there for a few minutes, and she said, "I don't know when your dad will be home. He is late, so we will eat and put something away for him." So, we started eating. We had just begun, and we heard the door open, and we all got up from the table and met my dad in the living room. We were all asking if they were going back to work, and he said yes! My younger brother and I were jumping up and down and he was saying we could get something for Christmas. All of us were happy. My dad said they had to do a lot of things before they could start the mines up, so he would start work on Friday. The week went fast, and my dad came home Friday, and he was very happy that he had been in the dark mines that day. My older brother told my mom and dad he never wanted to work in the coal mines and my dad asked him what he wanted to do, and he said he wanted to go where our oldest brother went who came home from the war and got a job. He said, "I can't make money here that I can live on." Dad said, "I understand."

"SATURDAY"

My aunt and my brother are working today. My brother said he made a counter for the man at the whiskey store and had to go paint it and do some other things today, and my aunt said she was getting off early so she could go see her little boy and she told my mom she would eat at my grandmother's house and not to worry about her eating. When she left; it seemed like we were alone....

I asked my mom, "What are we going to do when my aunt leaves, when her husband gets out of prison, and then our older brother leaves to get a job?" My mom said, "We will have to make it and we can since your dad's working. So, don't worry."

My dad got his carbide headlamp he wears on his hat in the mines and shined it up and his clothes and hard toed boots he kept in a locker at the mines. He brought his clothes home once a week for my mom to wash and she had to wash them out in a tub they were so black from the coal. She would rinse them and then wash them in the washing machine. They never looked totally clean, but that's all you could do with them. My mom always worried that my dad's life would be taken in the coal mines. He had many friends who had broken backs and crushed legs and feet from coal falling on them. My dad had a cut on his forehead and a small one near his left cheek and the scars were purplish black from the coal flying back when he used the pick to get the coal out. The people who treated them for injuries couldn't get the coal washed out of the cuts and it stayed in the scars. We see these scars on many of the miners' faces. My dad told us he was back in the lower part of the mines working again. Some of the lower areas were only eighteen inches high and the miners had to scoot on their bellies to pick the coal out and shovel it and other miners would get it to the coal cars that were on rails, and they pushed them out when they were filled up. I asked my dad why the coal didn't fall in on them all over and he said, "It does in some places; but we have jacks and short logs holding it up in different areas." I said, "I don't want you to go in there." He said he had to. We were always getting funeral notices from different mines at least two or three times a year, and all the miners tried to attend, and they helped the families of the deceased. My aunt and my brother came home afterwards. We had eaten supper, but my mom put food back for them as she always did. My brother ate, but my aunt said she ate at my grandmother's, and she was fine.

My older brother popped us some popcorn after he ate supper. We liked for him to do that in the evening. It was snowing outside, and we were all eating popcorn. My aunt told my mom she told my grandmother about the baby, and I said, "What baby?" My mom told us she would have another baby soon. I said, "I hope it's a girl." She said, "I don't know." We kept eating the popcorn until it was gone, and my mom told us to get ready for bed. My aunt helped us and tucked us in. They stayed up talking and listening to the news on the radio.

We all slept in later than usual. It was Sunday morning, and my mom was frying bacon. We hadn't smelled that in a long time. I got up and looked out the window hoping it had snowed a few more inches, but it didn't. It barely covered the ground. I asked my mom where she got the bacon from, and she said my aunt brought it from my grandmother's. Some neighbor had killed their hog and gave them bacon and ribs, and my aunt knew we liked bacon and brought us some. We were happy to have the bacon with our gravy, eggs and biscuits. It was a real treat! My aunt and mom started cleaning up the kitchen and we got dressed and sat in the living room with my dad and older brother. My dad said he heard a car outside, and I got up and said, "It's two cars, daddy." They were driving up to the house. It was the sheriff and the constable. They came in and the sheriff took three cases of beer to his car and the constable brought four cases of beer in for us to keep. I saw them giving my dad some money and told my mom. She told me to quit talking about it and not say anything to anyone. I said OK.

We all sat back down in the living room and continued talking and my older brother said, "There is another car coming to the house. It's the man who owned the business.", and he was right. The man was knocking on the door and my dad said, "Come in." The man didn't look very happy. He said, "We can't open the place back up. They blew it up about 3 am this morning and I'm sure it was the same people that had done it before. There's nothing we can do; but I'll keep in touch with you. The neighbor told us the time she heard the explosion, that's how I know the time."

We were all shocked because that's a place we lived before. The man said, "They threw the dynamite through the windows. I'm glad none of us were there." My dad said, "Me, too." The man said the blocks were blown all over. My older brother looked sad. The man said he would come back to see us, and he left. My dad said we will drive up there and see it for the last time, so we all went up there and the man was right. The blocks were blown all over and were in pieces. It was sad for us to see it and we got out of there quickly. It was a relief to get back home. My mom looked at my dad and said, "We could have been there." My dad nodded his head yes. My mom said we don't need to talk about it anymore and told me and my younger brother not to tell anyone and we said OK.

"BACK TO WORK AND THINKING OF CHRISTMAS"

We were all up early Monday morning. My dad left the house first, then my aunt and older brother left for their jobs; me and my younger brother asked my mom how many days until Christmas, and she said eight days. We asked, "Will we get anything?" She said my dad and all the miners would get paid in advance before Christmas so they could have money for Christmas and their families. I asked how they did that, and she said they will work it out, don't worry. I said OK. My mom told us to get shoes on and hurry or we would miss the school bus, so we hurried out the door. We were so happy to get to school and we felt better knowing our dad was back at work. It was a happy day for all the kids at school whose fathers were back at work.

The teachers decorated the school windows and put wreaths in them. The week was passing fast, and we were all anxious to get time off from school for a few days before Christmas until after New Years Day. It was Friday and we were going home as our Christmas break started. The teacher gave us all some chocolate candy and a Christmas card to take home with us. We were embarrassed. None of us had anything for our teacher. I think she understood. We all rushed to get on the bus. We were happy to get home and have a lot of days off. My dad wasn't home yet; but my mom was making dinner. She said my dad would get a check today and she was right. My dad cashed the check before he came home and handed it to my mom and said it was Christmas money. My aunt and older brother came home, and they had money from the liquor store man he gave them for Christmas. My mom said she would go with my aunt and older brother Christmas shopping and my dad would stay home with me, my younger brother, and baby brother. I asked if I could go with them, and mom said no because I had to help my dad watch my baby brother. My aunt told us our grandmother was cooking Christmas dinner for all of us Tuesday evening. We were happy to hear that because we didn't see them very often and when my dad ran the business, we really missed seeing them, because we didn't have time to go. My grandfather wouldn't bring them to see us because he didn't like to be around people drinking.

It seemed like a long day and my aunt, mom and older brother had been gone for several hours. I asked my dad what time they would be back, and he said he didn't know, but they had to buy groceries and it's three o'clock now. My brothers wanted something to eat, and my dad let us eat a small bowl of corn flakes and he said they will cook when they come home. He washed the bowls and put them away and it was four o'clock and my dad was looking out and saw them coming home. They backed the car up to the front steps and opened the trunk, and it was full of wrapped Christmas presents. We were excited, but disappointed we couldn't see what was in the packages. My aunt and older brother unloaded the back of the car. It was all groceries. We hadn't had that many in a long time. My mom put the presents under the little tree my older brother had cut down in the mountains. I asked my aunt if she wrapped all the presents and she said no, the stores wrapped them free for them. They were all pretty with different colored paper and ribbons on them and some of them were for her little boy and the grandparents. My mom said we could open ours Tuesday morning, and they would take the others to our grandparents' house.

My aunt and mom had bought hot dogs, buns, and canned chili for us and they made that, and fried potatoes and canned green beans and we loved eating all of that. My aunt quickly washed the dishes and let us count the presents we had, and we were all really tired. My mom told us to get ready for bed and we did, and our baby brother went to bed. He had been running and playing all day and was tired. My mom let me, and my younger brother stay up longer than usual, but told us not to wake our baby brother or we would be in trouble. My younger brother went to sleep sitting on the sofa and my mom said for me to go to bed and my mom carried him to bed. The adults stayed up as usual and I don't know when they went to bed.

"TWO DAYS BEFORE CHRISTMAS"

We were all anxious. It had been a long time since we had anything new; when you don't have much, it doesn't take much to make you happy. We were staying on good behavior because we knew our mom would make us wait until Christmas to open our gifts. We were all together; none of them were at work. My mom and aunt were baking a large cake to take to our grandmother's house. My dad and older brother were washing the car. The temperature was about 65 degrees and that wasn't unusual. Many of our winters were mild. The tops of the mountains were white sometimes with snow, but we would have sunshine and mild temperatures. We seldom had a white Christmas, but when we did, it was a deep snow. We were all feeling happy we had plenty to eat and gifts to open. My mom told me and my younger brother to take our baths after dinner because tomorrow was Christmas Eve, and we would get to open our gifts. So, my aunt helped us hurry up as usual, and we were happy to go to bed early so we could get up early.

"CHRISTMAS EVE"

I was the first one up this morning. It was seven a.m., and I was anxious to see what we all got for Christmas. I was moving the gifts around hoping they would hear me and get up. My mom and my aunt got up at the same time and came into the living room and asked me what I was doing. I said, "Looking at the gift packages." My mom said she had to cook breakfast before we opened the gifts. My aunt started getting everything together and they were frying bacon, and that smell woke everyone up, except my baby brother. My dad said he would get him up and bring him to eat and let him open his gifts first so he would be happy.

We all washed our hands, and my dad seated us at the table and my mom and aunt served the food. We were happy to have bacon, eggs, gravy and biscuits, again. We all ate a little faster than usual. We wanted to see our gifts. We all were back in the living room and my dad handed my baby brother all his gifts at once and he started opening them and smiling. He was a really good little boy. They bought him a train set with the tracks and my dad put it together and he loved watching it go around the tracks. He also had some wind-up cars and new clothes. He was happy. My younger brother got a cowboy outfit with guns and a holster and a cowboy hat, and some new clothes. He was really happy. They told me to open mine. I got a doll, a necklace, bracelet, and two dresses, and I was very happy. My aunt and my mom told my older brother to open his and they bought him a new belt, two pairs of Levi's, two shirts and he was smiling and said, "This is what I needed." My mom opened hers and my aunt and brother bought her a set of dishes and two dresses and a new tablecloth. She was really happy because the old tablecloth was worn out and had several holes in it. My dad and my aunt opened their presents at the same time. My mom bought my aunt a new purse and shoes and two dresses and she was really happy. My mom, aunt and older brother bought my dad a new coat for work, and he got two pairs of pants and two shirts and a new lunch bucket. He didn't expect that but the one he had was really old and dented from being in the mines and he was happy.

We all were grateful that we got everything we wanted and needed at the time.

"GRATEFUL CHRISTMAS DAY"

We all got up early and ate a quick breakfast and got new clothes out to wear to our grandmother's house; my mom said my baby brother could take his small toys with him and that would keep him happy. My aunt got the gifts out for her little boy and put them in the car. She didn't buy the grandparents anything. They knew dad had just got back to work and they didn't want anything; my grandmother just wanted to have us all there for dinner and to be with us. My aunt carried the big cake she and my mom made to the car. It was decorated beautifully, and they covered it with wax paper, and she said she would hold it in her lap so it wouldn't get messed up and she did. We were all in the car and on our way. They lived about twenty miles from us, and we were soon getting out of the car. My aunt carried the cake, and my mom carried the gifts that my aunt had got for her little boy. We were all happy to see each other. My aunt's little boy had grown a lot, and he was still a very good child. My grandmother took him to church with her all the time. She was good to him.

"GOOD FOOD AT GRANDMA'S"

They opened the gifts they had for each other, and my aunt's little boy opened the gifts she bought him. She got him a train set with tracks like my baby brother got and a very small tricycle. My grandfather put the

train set together and her little boy was so happy with it. He was pushing
the tricycle around on the floor and he was very happy.

My grandmother had some strawberry punch and gave all the
adults a glass of it with real frozen strawberries in it, and the children
got paper cups with the punch in it. We all liked that. My grandmother
had been up since five a.m. roasting a turkey and a large ham. It smelled
really good in the house. She had made mashed potatoes, green beans,
and a large platter of salad that was something we never ate at home.
She had baked a large apple pie and a pecan pie and showed it to me.
She knew I loved apple pie. We all were seated in the living room and
talking. My grandfather told my dad he was happy he didn't run that
business anymore. My dad told him, "I had to do something with no
money coming in, it was hard to live." My mom said, "Let's not talk
about that, let's be happy."

My grandmother said, "Everything will be ready in about an hour
and a half, it will be about three o'clock when I serve it, and I will give you
all some to take home for tomorrow and you won't have to cook dinner."

My grandfather had horseshoe stakes driven in the ground outside
and it was fairly warm. He asked if my mom, dad, and older brother
wanted to pitch some horseshoes. They all went outside to play, and
my mom said she hadn't done that in years. They enjoyed being out on
Christmas Day. My grandmother had me set the table. It was a long table my grandfather had made. Once the table was set, my grandmother
called them to come in. They all were washing their hands, and my
grandmother seated the adults facing each other, and she had a highchair for my aunt's little boy. My younger brother and I sat beside each
other, and my mom held my baby brother on her lap to help him eat. My
grandmother gave thanks to God for our meal, and for all of us being
together. We all loved her cooking. She was an old-fashioned cook. She
made everything herself. That was one of the best dinners we had in a
long time. I think we all sat at the table for about two hours talking. My
mom let my baby brother down after she wiped his hands good, and my
aunt put her little boy to bed. He was tired.

We kept sitting at the table for dessert. My grandmother cut the pies
into several pieces, and she served us all what we wanted. My aunt cut
the big cake into small pieces, and I had a piece of apple pie and a small

piece of cake. My mom poured the coffee for the adults and the children had milk. We all ate our dessert and went back to the living room and sat down. My aunt told my grandparents her husband would be getting out of prison soon and she was going back to Baltimore with him. My grandmother looked sad over that. We loved my aunt's little boy and that would be hard for her to give him up. I began to dread the day my aunt would leave. She helped my mom with everything. My dad thanked our grandparents for the dinner and asked if we were ready to go home and we said yes; and thanked our grandparents. My grandmother had got us a bag of leftovers ready to go and we were happy to get it. Everything was so good. We hugged them bye and went to the car. They all came out and waved us bye.

We were all tired and wanted to go to bed early. My dad drove us through the small town on the way home and let us look at the Christmas lights, then we went home and got ready for bed.

"THE DAY AFTER CHRISTMAS; A SAD DAY"

We got up later than usual. We were all tired and none of us wanted a big breakfast, so my mom made coffee for the adults and hot chocolate for us kids, and my aunt made pancakes and we had maple syrup on them, and we really liked it. We all finished breakfast, and my mom told us all to go to the living room and she washed the dishes.

My aunt was talking about how she would be leaving soon and would be with her husband and little boy and we all were sad faced about it. We couldn't imagine her not being with us. We all went through so much together. She told my mom she hoped the baby was a girl because I had all brothers, and I was outnumbered by all the boys. My mom had said we would have to wait and see. My older brother said he would soon be going to stay with our oldest brother so he could get a job and buy him a car. This was a sad day for us. It seemed like our family was all breaking up. We went through all those tragic things together and somehow; we didn't want to let go of them. They seemed sad also because they loved us. My dad said let's talk about this some other time. He seen how me, and my younger brother, were about to cry. Our baby brother was playing with his toys, and he was happy. My dad got a puzzle out that we hadn't put together in a long time and got us all involved in doing that together and we forgot about anyone leaving and we finished that big puzzle in about two hours. We all took it apart and put it away. My dad and older brother went outside to get wood for the fireplace and stove. My mom and aunt went back into the kitchen and were getting the leftovers ready for dinner and mom washed the new dishes she got for Christmas and set the table with them. They were so pretty, and they made everything look so good. It was like we had Christmas dinner again.

My younger brother and I had to take a bath and put our pajamas on, but my mom said we could stay up later because we didn't have to go to school until the end of next week. We were starting back on a Friday. It was parent-teacher conferences, and it was a half day of school for us. My mom and dad came to talk to our teacher in the afternoon and she sent a note to our teacher that they would take us home, so we got to go outside. When our parents came and were talking to the teacher, it wasn't that long. We both had good grades and my mom said the teacher said we were good students, and that was good. We got in the car and headed home. My dad stopped by the post office and got the mail and handed it to my mom. She was going through the mail and said my aunt's husband had written a letter to her and I asked if we could read it and she said, "No, we don't read other people's mail." My dad was turning off on the dirt road, which led up to our house.

"LOADING THE BEER"

When we topped the little hill, we could see the sheriff's and the constable's cars. My older brother was loading beer in their cars and my dad pulled the car beside them and we all got out. My mom took us into the house, and my dad stayed outside talking to them with my older brother.

My aunt already prepared everything so my mom could cook, and mom thanked her. My dad and older brother went to the living room and had all us kids sit in there with them. I heard my mom tell my aunt she got a letter from her husband, and she told her to read it and she would get dinner together. I heard her tell my mom he was getting out of prison early on "good behavior", and he would be out in seven days. I didn't want my mom to know I was listening, but it gave me a sad feeling. My dad and brother were talking about the sheriff and constable. They begged my dad to let them bring forty cases of beer a week and my dad told them he could only put it under the floor, and it would get dirty. They said OK and they were supposed to pay him more money and I asked how much, and my dad said, "You're not supposed to talk about this to anyone." I said OK.

"AUNT LEAVING US"

My mom quickly set the table and the rest of the family came in. We all sat down, and my aunt was telling my mom she would help her clean the house really good next week and scrub the porches if it's not too cold. My mom said, "don't worry about that." We were all thinking about her leaving, and it wasn't a happy thought. We all went through so much we became like soldiers wanting to help each other and there was an edge of anxiety over the fright we had gone through. My aunt told my mom she had to go tell the egg man she had to quit work in the morning. "I hope he can get someone else to help him. He is so nice," she said. This week passed really fast, and New Years was over with. My aunt was getting everything ready for her to leave. She had run to the egg man and told him bye, and he thanked her and gave her ten dollars as a gift; she said he was sad she was leaving. We were back to school this week and my dad was back to work.

We came home from school and my mom was letting my older brother iron some clothes while she cooked, and he was doing a good job. He said he had to learn because he would be taking care of himself when he got a job and mom said that was true.

My dad came home, and my mom and aunt were setting the table. They woke my baby brother up. He had fallen asleep on the sofa, but he woke up in a good mood. We were all talking as we sat down, about my aunt leaving and she said she would come back and see us. We were happy to hear that. My younger brother and I asked if we could take Friday off from school. That's when my aunt was leaving for my grandmother's house when her husband would come to the bus station, and she would pick him up and they would leave for Baltimore the next day. We all were tired and worried about my aunt leaving so we went to bed a little early. My mom got up a little late the next morning. She forgot to set the clock and we all had to get ready fast for us to go to school and my dad to work. My dad left and we hurried to the bus stop and caught the bus. The day passed very fast. Our teacher kept us busy, and we were on the school bus going home again. When we got home, our aunt and our mom had scrubbed the porches and were moving furniture around in the living room and told us we could sit on the swing on the front porch. It was nice weather. It seemed more like spring than winter. My older brother wasn't home. He went to see the man at the liquor store and would be back soon.

"AUNT MAKING WHAT WE LOVED MOST"

My younger brother started aggravating my aunt knocking on the front door and hiding when my aunt would come to the door and she told him not to do that again and he waited a few minutes and done it again, and she was getting mad at him and told him to stop it. About a half hour later the sheriff came by, and he was knocking on the door and my aunt yelled out, "You little son of a bitch, if you knock again, I will come out and bust your ass!" The sheriff stood back from the door and my brother yelled to my aunt, "It's not me. It's the sheriff." She came to the door and told him she was so sorry, but my younger brother kept knocking on the door and aggravating them, and she was so embarrassed. I never heard her say many bad words. She tried to be nice always. The sheriff got the beer and was leaving. We saw our dad coming home and he and the sheriff stopped and talked to each other and then my dad came home. My dad went into the house and my mom said we could come in. I smelled chili cooking and dad asked if we were having hot dogs and my aunt said, yes. I wanted to make them for you before I must leave. My older brother came home. Someone had given him a ride and he said the liquor store man said he would have some work for him in the spring, but he said he will be gone then. We were sad when they talked about leaving. It was Thursday night, and we knew my aunt would leave us tomorrow to go to our grandparents' house. It was much closer to the bus station where she would pick her husband up and they would leave for Baltimore from there. None of the family wanted her husband around. He always caused trouble, that's why they were leaving from the bus station, and she said her husband's former boss was bringing him back again and letting them stay with him and his wife until he could rent a place for them. My mom put all the food on the table and told us to get ready to eat and then be seated, which we did.

We all appreciated my aunt's home-made chili for the hot dogs. We always ate all of it. We finished dinner and my mom told my aunt to go sit down with all of us in the living room and she did. She was talking about her little boy and how she could spend all the time with him but dreaded taking him from our grandmother.

"ANXIETY"

My mom finally came into the living room with us. We all seemed to have some anxiety about tomorrow, but my dad was good at changing the subject. He didn't want us to worry. Our baby brother was happy, still playing with his toys. I asked my mom if me and my younger brother still got to take tomorrow off from school, and she said yes. My younger brother and I took our own baths with no help from my aunt or mom. We began to see if we could be independent, and we liked that. We put our pajamas on and came back and sat on each side of my aunt. She was smiling at us and told us that we both were growing up and someday we would go to college and have good jobs. My mom said, "I hope so." My aunt was tired and said she was going to bed early so she could be up early in the morning. She already had her clothes and everything ready. My younger brother said he would go to bed early so he could be up early with our aunt, and I said, "I'm going to bed so I can be up early, too." My mom, dad, and older brother stayed up. Our baby brother was asleep on the sofa and my dad carried him to bed. I remember that night very well. I really wanted to go to sleep because I felt like I was about to cry. I was counting to one hundred quietly trying to get to sleep and finally, I was asleep.

"SADDEST DAY IN OUR LIVES"

My mom, dad, and aunt were all up at five a.m. My mom was frying bacon and potatoes and making a big breakfast. It was soon done and on the table. We all took our seats and then our older brother got up and washed his hands quickly and sat down. My aunt told my mom she appreciated her making all the food. My dad was the first up from the table. He had to go to work, and he looked sad. He gave my aunt a big hug and said, "I wish you the best", and handed her some money. She said, "I don't need it", but he insisted. He also thanked her for everything she had done for us and with us. My mom didn't wake up our baby brother. She said he will cry too much and it's too early. My older brother carried all my aunt's things to her car. My aunt said she would be leaving in a few minutes and said that as soon as she has an address, she will write us a letter. She went to kiss our baby brother bye, and my mom said don't wake him. She came back to the living room and hugged my mom, older brother, and then hugged and kissed my younger brother and she had tears in her eyes. My younger brother and I were hanging on to her and crying, "Please don't leave us." My mom and older brother had tears running down their faces. It was very emotional. My mom took us by the hand and walked us to the sofa to sit down. My aunt said, "I love all of you." We were all crying and told her we loved her, too. She walked out the door and we all were waving and crying. Mom closed the door and said, "God bless her."

We could only wait for my dad to come home from work. My mom woke our baby brother up and he asked where our aunt was, and my mom said she went to see her little boy and she told us to say the same thing. She didn't want him crying. My younger brother said she was our other mom and our mom agreed. My older brother said he would chop some more wood and put it under the front porch, and my mom said, "Don't put it under the house. The beer is stacked there." He said, "I know." He went out and was chopping the wood and my mom said my younger brother and I could help her cook before dad came home and we liked that. The day seemed to pass very slowly.

My older brother finally came in. He had chopped up a lot of wood and put it under the porch. His shoes and hands were dirty and from picking up the wood blocks to chop. The blocks were dirty from us having to burn the coal in the fireplace and the stove, and the smoke was sooty and settled on the wood blocks by the house. Mom told him to take a bath before our dad came home and he did; he came into the kitchen after his bath, and he smelled so good. I asked him what he put on his face, and he said the aftershave our aunt bought him for Christmas. We all loved the smell of it and our younger brother said, "Put some on my face", and he did. Our older brother had been growing much taller in the past two years and his hair was dark brown but looked black when he put hair oil on it. His eyes were blue. Everyone thought he was good looking, and I think he is, too. He was always flexing his muscles and smiling. We all loved him. My dad finally came home from work, and he had a small bandage on his forehead. He said a piece of coal hit him when they were picking it out and he was bleeding, so he had to be taken to the hospital and be sutured. My mom said, "You will have another coal scar on your face." That's what everyone called them because they couldn't get the coal marking out of the wound. It stayed dark bluish. Most of the miners had those marks on their faces. It was a hazard to the job. My older brother looked at my dad and said, "That is another reason I don't want to work in the mines." My dad said, "I hope you never have to."

"DAD MAY HAVE ROCK DUST (BLACK LUNG)"

We all sat down to eat, and we were looking at each other. Our aunt's seat was empty, and we were missing her already. My mom was getting bigger in her abdomen. She would be having the baby in a few months, and I was still hoping for a girl. Finally, we all got up from the table and my mom said she would wash the dishes and then come into the living room with us afterwards. My dad looked tired, and he had begun to cough a lot. He said he may have rock dust in the lungs; we were hoping he was wrong, and my mom came in the living room as she heard what he had said and told him he needed to be checked for it to find out, and he said he would.

"STILL KEEPING BEER FOR THE POLICE"

My older brother walked outside, and he saw the sheriff coming, so he came back in. He said, "He's coming for the beer. I'll load it for him." My mom told us to stay on the sofa until he leaves, and we did. My brother got six cases of beer and loaded it in his car, and he left. My dad and older brother stayed outside talking for a while and I asked my mom who is going to drink all that beer and she said, "I told you not to talk about that and not to tell anyone." I said OK. My dad and older brother came back in. They were talking about someone's home that had been raided. The sheriff said the state took a man and his wife to jail. My mom said, "I hope that never happens here", and told my dad, "We have to stop this." He said, "When I get a little money ahead, we can." My mom asked my dad to take us to see her aunt who lived in town. We hadn't seen her for a long time since we started the business. My mom was best friends with her daughter, who was her first cousin, and they went to the movies together and visited each other often, but she left with some relatives and went to Detroit and got a job and came back to see us and she looks so pretty. She told my mom she was getting married to a young man from the middle east, and she told her mom and dad he was a Muslim, and they didn't want her to marry him, but she went back to Detroit and married him anyway. We continued driving to the aunt's house and when we arrived, my mom's uncle answered the door and said, "This is a pleasant surprise." He told us to come on in. We were all happy to see each other but my mom's aunt seemed a bit sad. She seated us all at the kitchen table and took a large chocolate cake out of the refrigerator and cut it and gave us all a slice and poured my mom and dad a cup of coffee and all of us kids drank milk with the cake, and it was good. We all continued to sit at the table because the aunt wanted to show my mom something and it was a yellow piece of paper with black writing on it. My mom said it was a telegram from her daughter's husband in Detroit and it said her daughter was in the hospital in Detroit with a brain tumor in her head, and they were going to operate on her brain next Wednesday and asked her to come there to be with her. Mom's aunt sent a telegram back and said she would be there. The aunt started crying and told my mom that they had a little girl about two years old before they got married and her daughter told her about it, and she kept it a secret. It was like a disgrace for a woman to have a baby out of wedlock during that time and her parents were very religious, and she said she didn't want her daughter disgraced. My mom said, "I understand." She was sad hearing that. The aunt said, "Let's all go back into the living room." We all were seated, and my mom asked her aunt how she was going to Detroit, and she said she was getting a bus ticket and leaving Tuesday morning, and the surgery would be Wednesday afternoon. She could see her daughter before surgery. She was very hurt about this and told my mom and dad she would let them know when she came back, and my mom said, "Please do." We all got up and got ready to go home and mom's aunt noticed that my mom was going to have a baby and she said, "It's time to have a little girl." My mom said, "Whatever God gives us." We all said goodbye, and the aunt was crying when we left and said she would let us know soon as she could.

We left quietly and my mom said she hoped she'd make it through this. It was almost dark when we got home, so we got ready for bed. We were all tired and said good night and went to bed.

"Sunday morning", and we all slept in, but my mom was first up and had breakfast ready and told us all to get up and we did. The night before was still on mom's mind and we all could tell it. Mom said she had been praying for her cousin to live to talk to her mom, but she said God only knows. We all got up from the table being quiet and sat in the living room and my mom went back into the kitchen and cleaned it. My mom's aunt and uncle had other children married but living in another state and they had one daughter at home finishing her last year of high school, but she was with a friend at the movies, so we didn't see her. The day passed very fast, and we got our school clothes ready for tomorrow and we were anxious to go back. There were a lot of things happening and going to school got us away from everything. My mom made us hot dogs trying to keep us happy. That was a favorite with us, we had no trouble eating them. We were all anxious to just go to bed. We sat up for a short time but went to bed quick.

"EMOTIONAL EXPERIENCES"

We were all up-smelling bacon my mom was frying, of course baby brother was still sleeping. My mom served my dad because he had to leave early, within a few minutes. We were all eating and wishing our aunt was with us. We went out the door quickly and told my mom bye. The school bus was in sight, so we ran up to the bus stop. Our neighbor friends were laughing because we were almost late.

We were all talking, and we were at the school when we looked up, we all quickly got off the bus. It was good to see our friends after our emotional experiences. I thought about my mom, it was like she couldn't get away from it.

Our day at school went really fast but it was a good break for us. The day passed quickly, and we were again getting on the school bus going home. I was anxious to comfort my mom. We got off the school bus and ran home. My mom and older brother were in the kitchen. She taught him how to make cornbread. He always loved it and wanted to know how to make it. We washed our hands and my mom let me set the table, and my older brother was cutting the cornbread as my dad was walking through the door. The bread looked just like my mom baked it. We all sat down and ate together, and we wished our aunt was there. Our baby brother asked when she was coming back, and my mom said she didn't know and winked at me, so I would be quiet.

My older brother said he would wash the dishes and I could dry them, and he would put them away, and he did; and my mom thanked us. We all sat down in the living room and my dad was listening to the news on the radio. Our baby brother was good, and always playing with his toys.

"MOM'S AUNT LEAVING FOR DETROIT ON A BUS"

My mom reminded us of her aunt leaving in the morning, "Tuesday", on a bus to Detroit to see her daughter before the brain surgery and she said we all should say a prayer for all of them tonight. We all said OK. I said mine as soon as I went to bed, and I think they all said one because we all loved the daughter of mom's aunt and wished the best for her. We all were tired and went to bed. My dad stayed up a few minutes longer, but I could see the light was turned out in the living room and everyone was quiet. It was dark in the mountains at night but if you stayed up late, the wild cats would scream in the early morning hours, and they sounded like a woman screaming. I finally fell asleep. I had anxiety about my mom's aunt going to see her daughter. My mom had to wake me up, I was so tired. My brother was already up and dressed. We were eating corn flakes for breakfast, so it was quick. My dad left for work. He only had a cup of coffee. All of us were tired. We just wanted time to pass and have a good day, every day. My younger brother and I were racing to get to the bus stop a little early. We all had some anxiety, and everything was different since our aunt left. We talked to our neighbor friends at the bus stop for a few minutes and then the bus came, and we quickly boarded. Our bus driver was a very nice man. He joked with all of us; and we all liked him. He taught us to get seated fast because he was a teacher in our small town, and he took the bus back and taught classes in town. We were well disciplined in school. Our parents were strict and so were our teachers, and that made our schools really good. We were soon boarding the school bus going home and we were still anxious because our mom was worrying about her cousin who was her best friend growing up, and she couldn't imagine her having brain surgery and she said a lot of people die from that. I said, "Maybe she will be OK." She said she hoped so.

My dad was a little late coming home. He stopped by the post office and got our mail. There was a letter from our oldest brother and my mom said she would read it to us after dinner. We hurried up eating wanting to hear what our older brother had to tell us. My mom began reading it to us. He said he was happy, making money, had his own place and a good job. My mom slowed down reading and I said, "Why are you reading so slow?" She said, "You might not want to hear all of this." We said we wanted to hear it all, so she kept reading and he was asking our older brother if he wanted to come stay with him and get a good job, and if so, he would come at the end of February because they begin hiring then. We had sad faces when we heard that. She finished the letter and said, "Your brother needs to go and get a good job and buy him a car and make a good living." Our older brother said he would come back often to see us. Mom and dad told us that we will grow up someday and will want a good job, too; and that there's nothing here but coal mines and I know that you don't want that. My mom said she didn't want that for us. My mom cleaned up the kitchen and we all went to the living room and talked, and then got ready for bed. We all said good night, and no one wanted to stay up.

"WEDNESDAY"

This day began like most of the others. My mom looked really tired, but she had breakfast on the table for us and my dad was in a hurry. He had to go to a meeting for safety, so he left quickly and said he would see us after work. I noticed my mom didn't set a plate on the table for herself, but she was drinking coffee. I asked her what was wrong, and she said,

"I didn't sleep well last night." I asked her, "Are you worrying about your cousin?" She said, "Yes." I said I prayed last night for her, and she said she did, too. My older brother said, "I hope she makes it. She was always so much fun and everyone loved her." My mom rushed us out the door, we were about to be late for the bus. We boarded the bus, and we were talking to our friends and time went fast and we were at school so quickly, and we were happy to be there. Soon, we were back on the bus and going home. I told my brother our mom may have news about her cousin. I hope that it's good. We were running up the hill and the sheriff and the constable were there, and my older brother was loading beer cases in their cars. We ran in the house and my mom was cooking and seemed OK. I asked, "Have you heard anything about your cousin?" She said, "No. Maybe that means she's OK." I said that I hoped so. My older brother set the table for my mom, and they were talking, and my dad came in and he asked if she had heard anything about her cousin, and she said no. He said that maybe she is OK, and my mom just nodded her head. My Older brother told us, "Wash your hands and come to the table." We all sat down and finished our dinner. Our baby brother had outgrown his highchair and was now sitting on a stool, but he was happy. My dad led my baby brother into the living room and told us to come with him; our mom and older brother cleaned the kitchen up then came in with us and my dad asked my mom if she wanted to go see her cousin's dad and see if he knew anything about his daughter. My mom said no because they said they would let her know. None of us had phones. My mom said they should get another telegram, so we would have to wait and see. My dad suggested he take us for a ride by the river and we said yes; so, we all went to the car, got in and left. We loved going. They let us out and we all walked to the bank of the river, and it was clear, and we watched the fish swimming and seen the crayfish on the sandy bottom. We all liked watching them. We stayed there for about an hour and the sun was beginning to go down. Dad said it would be getting dark soon, so we all got back in the car and went home. My mom told me and my younger brother to get ready for bed and put our pajamas on, and we did really fast. My dad turned the radio on for the news, and they were listening to it. Our baby brother was playing with his toys, as usual. It was late evening, and the sun was going down over the mountain; it was a nice day and warm. We only needed a sweater.

We had a mild winter as many of our winters were, and we liked it a lot. My dad was still listening to the news on the radio, and we didn't hear a car pull up to the house, but there was a knock on the door and my dad opened the door and it was mom's cousin's father, and his neighbors who drove him to see us. He was crying and handed my mom the telegram he got. She was reading it and crying. The neighbors said he got it earlier and they stayed with him. He was so distraught for a few hours, then he asked them to drive him to our house, and they did. We were all very "upset". My older brother read the telegram to us. Her mom sent it. She said the bus was late and I didn't get to see her before she went to surgery, but they told her I was on my way. My mom was still crying, and we were crying. Our older brother popped some popcorn and took all of us kids into the kitchen so they could talk in the living room. My brother took them some popcorn in the living room, but no one at it. My mom wanted to know where her cousin would be buried, and her dad said he wanted her buried in their family graveyard but didn't know if the husband would allow it. I heard them talking about the little girl and her grandfather said they were going to ask if they could keep her, but they didn't know yet.

Shortly after that was said, the neighbors said they had to get home because he had to work in the morning, so all of them gathered at the front door and they told us bye and my mom's uncle told us all to come see him tomorrow and he would have more information, so my mom said OK, and closed the door. She told us we had to get to bed quickly. We were all so tired, we went to bed quietly. We all got up Thursday a.m. and my dad left ahead of us to work, after breakfast. I asked my mom if we could stay home and she said no, because they will have to take us out of school for the funeral, so I said OK. We went on to school and I kept on thinking about the little girl not having a mother and tears were rolling down my cheeks, and the teacher called me up to her desk and asked what was wrong. I told her, and she knew the family, as most everyone in the small town knew each other, and she said she was very sorry to hear that and that she would probably attend the funeral. The day went really fast, and we were home so quick, it seemed like a half day of school. My dad looked really tired when he came home. My older brother and my mom had all the clothes washed and ironed and dinner made. My mom said, "We have to stay ahead of things so we will be ready for the funeral." My dad nodded, yes. We all were helping put everything away after the dishes were done. My dad told me and my brother to go take our baths and put on tomorrow's school clothes, so we could go see mom's uncle and give him some support, so we did everything we were told to do, and we were ready to go. My mom had made a large chocolate cake to take to their house and when we arrived, there were several of her uncle's neighbors there with him and they had brought food for the family, which was customary when someone had passed away; people were kind and most knew each other. My mom's uncle handed her another telegram, and it said her aunt would be home Friday evening and that the daughter died in surgery and that the brain tumor was too big to remove, and she had to go to the morgue to see her body, and they had tied her head up in a scarf because they had shaved her head for the surgery. Her daughter's husband went with her to the morgue and had to explain that her daughter had his brother's wife's name tied to her ankle because he didn't have insurance and they had to pass her off as his brother's wife, so she had the same last name, but was being called by his brother's wife's first name. My mom was upset to hear that, and she said, "She died under someone else's name", but she said, "Maybe they had to do it."

Dad was really tired, and he had fallen asleep in a chair there, and mom had woken him up so we could go home. Everyone was shaking hands with dad and mom's uncle said, "Please come back tomorrow." Dad said that we would. Dad felt sorry for him; he was always a good man. We had a quick breakfast the next morning, but it was good. Dad had already left. He has been very tired working hard and going to mom's uncle's house to try to cheer him up. Mom and dad always liked him. I was at school and the teacher asked if I knew when the funeral was, and I said no. She said she would listen to the radio, and they should talk about it, and I went back to my seat. She was grading papers.

When we got home, mom made hot dogs and chili. We were happy when we smelled it. Dad came home a little late and mom and I had to wash all the dishes and we got it done fast. Dad and mom had to get dressed fast, and she let us wear our school clothes. We arrived there quickly, and they cut us a lemon pie, and we loved it. Mom gave permission and said yes. We chose to have lemon pie, and it was really good and homemade. We thanked them and my mom had to wake our dad up again, as he was so tired. He got up and shook hands with everyone and we were heading home, and my mom was crying again, thinking about her cousin and the wrong name tag on her in the morgue. I asked my mom, "Did they have to do that?" She said, "Don't ever tell anyone about that." I said, "OK". Soon we were home, and happy to go to bed.

"IDENTIFICATION"

We all slept in. It was Saturday morning and we had to go back to my mom's aunt and uncle's house. My mom said she had to help her aunt explain to the mortician in our small town what had happened at the hospital in Michigan because the body was supposed to be shipped to him today. We all left the house and arrived at my mom's aunt and uncle's house, and her aunt was ready to go to the morgue with my mom, and my dad was driving them, and they left us with her uncle and all the neighbors were with them and we sat in the living room talking with them. They were so sweet, and we enjoyed talking with them. My mom, dad and her aunt arrived back about two hours later and they were in the kitchen talking about how the aunt had picked a dress to bury her daughter in, and they explained what had happened in Michigan with her identification and the funeral director told her mom since he knew the whole family and her daughter, and my mom and dad, everything would be OK, that he just had to sign for the body (corpse) that he received it and he would make things proper and for her mom not to worry. The body was supposed to arrive there today at four p.m., and her mom was to check back in with the funeral director tomorrow morning. My dad drove them back to her home where we were at, and her aunt said her son in law and the little granddaughter would be at her house later in the evening. My mom and dad offered for them to stay with us, but she said they would be with her for two nights, as that's all he could stay because he had to go back to work, and he wouldn't stay for the funeral. We didn't know if it was about his religion or what, but he said he wanted the little girl to see her mom in the coffin, and he was going to tell her she was "sleeping" so her mom agreed to this. We all soon departed and went home. We were really tired. The neighbor said they would drive them to the funeral home in the morning and they would set the day for the funeral; and we were supposed to come back tomorrow evening. We were all happy to get home. My mom and dad were really tired, more than us, and she made some soup and grilled cheese. We all ate and quickly cleaned up and went to the living room and my dad turned the radio on to hear the news. We were all quiet and wanted to rest. We all headed to bed after sitting for about two hours, he was, too. We slept in again; we were exhausted.

Finally, my mom got up and made pancakes and cereal for us and they had pancakes and coffee. My mom had us take our baths after breakfast and she washed some clothes and reminded us we had to stay clean to go in the evening back to the aunt's home. We said OK. Our older brother got the big puzzle out and took us into the kitchen to the table and we all were trying to put it together. We had about half of it done and we wanted to quit, so our older brother put it away; and we went in the living room and my older brother asked my mom and dad who was paying for the funeral, and my dad said he offered to give them some money toward it, but they refused and the aunt said the son in law's family had all gave money to him for that and the coffin and funeral cost six hundred dollars and all they had to buy was the family wreath for the coffin. My mom said they were really nice to do that. Our baby brother fell asleep on the sofa and our dad said let him sleep because we will all be tired again tonight. My mom said she was going to make us fried bologna sandwiches with cheese melted on it for a late lunch today because her aunt said her church was making a big dinner for everyone, and dessert, and whatever the people wanted to drink, so she told my mom not to feed us too much so we could eat with them. We all were sitting quietly, and we heard a car pull up to the house, and it was the sheriff wanting several cases of beer, and our older brother helped him load it into the car and our dad was talking to him. He said he was dropping off some to the constable and he paid my dad for both. In the meantime, our mom made the sandwiches and poured milk for us, and baby brother woke up and my mom washed his hands and put him on his stool at the table. We all quickly ate our sandwiches and my mom had them on paper plates, so she only had one pan and drinking glasses to wash, and everyone got quickly out of the kitchen. My dad was shining his shoes and wore his suit and tie, and we were all dressed as good as we could be. My dad told us we would leave in thirty minutes. We were all ready to go. My mom put a pillow in the car for our baby brother. He always fell asleep in the car when we were out in the evening. Finally, my dad was ready to go. He grabbed our baby brother and carried him to the car, and we were off to the aunt's house; we arrived before sundown and there were a lot of cars parked at their house. We all got out of the car and walked to the door with neighbors greeting us and we walked into the dining room. They had a long table with lots of warm foods and desserts at one end of the table and chairs all around the walls. They had paper plates and real silverware, and my mom's aunt was hugging her, and her eyes were very swollen. She had been crying a lot. They went and viewed their daughter's body, and she said the mortician had put a gown on her. They set the funeral for Wednesday at 11 a.m., and her son in law was taking the little girl to view her Tuesday, and all the people could view her, also. Mom told us to take a seat by the wall and we went and sat down, and our older brother got our food for us, and came to sit with us. We couldn't believe how much food the people made and brought to them. Everyone was eating and talking about how good the food was and the pies and cakes looked like professional chefs had made them. People in the mountains were very kind and loving toward their neighbors. We ate all the food we wanted and desserts. Everyone was so kind and had good hearts. The evening went by very fast. We were all talking, and it was dark. My dad told my mom we must leave in about thirty minutes, and she came and sat with us and said we would be leaving soon. We were really tired. My mom's aunt brought a big bag to her and said, "There's cake and a lot of cookies in it." She said she had nowhere to put the food; they brought so much. She told my mom she was going to ask several of them to take pies back to their refrigerators, and they could bring them back tomorrow. My dad came over and asked my mom if she was ready to go and she said yes. She told her aunt bye and her uncle, while my dad was still shaking hands with all the men and saying good night to everyone. We all left, and my mom was crying again. We got to see a lot of people we hadn't seen in a long time. It's like our lives had stopped after the businesses my dad run for the man had been burned down and blown up. It's like we were all traumatized. We didn't want to do anything we didn't have to do, but I was always wandering and wanted to go to town and see the little woman (the fortune teller) that I loved. She always made me feel whole again and told me good things. I also wanted to go back to the juke joint where they played live music there a lot and they were all nice, but my mom wouldn't let me mention it because she didn't want my dad drinking again. We arrived home from my mom's aunt's house, and we were tired, and we all went to bed. My mom was up early the next day making breakfast. My dad had to go to work, and I asked if me and my brother could take the day off from school and she said yes, and we were happy because we were tired.

Today, everyone would view my mom's cousin at the funeral home, and we all had to dress up again. The day went fast, and my dad was home quicker than usual, and my mom said we could have pie and cookies with milk, and we were all happy with that. My mom said after the viewing, we would go back to the house and her aunt said there would be more food and we could eat there. She said she didn't want to throw food away.

"SAD DAY"

We all were getting dressed and my dad sat down after he was dressed; he was very tired. My mom said they are letting everyone view the body along with family. My dad asked if we were all ready to go and we said yes. We all headed for the front door, and we were soon in the car and on our way. My mom said she would walk up to the coffin with us and for us to be quiet. We said OK. We finally were in town and cars were parked in front of the funeral home and everywhere. My dad had to park on another street, and it was crowded. We all got out of the car and were walking towards the funeral home and there was a line of people on the outside, but some were coming out, so we got in line, and it took about fifteen minutes for us to get in and my teacher came out and seen me. She talked to me and my mom and dad, briefly. My mom took me and my brother's hand to walk us up to the coffin. My dad and older brother walked up with our baby brother and when I seen her cousin in the coffin, I said out loud, "Mommy, they didn't fix her hair." She said to be quiet and whispered to me that they shaved her head for the brain surgery, and they put a turban on her head. My mom's aunt and the son in law and her uncle were talking to the funeral director and the little girl was sitting in a chair by them. We walked over by them, and they were asking if they could raise the vail that was draped over the coffin, so her little daughter could kiss her on the cheek and say good night because her dad was telling her that mommy was sleeping and the funeral director said yes, but to be careful and not to let go of her and he would hold the vail up for them; so he took her over to kiss her mom on the cheek and she said, "Good night mommy...I love you." It was heartbreaking. Everyone had tears in their eyes. Most people left to go to the aunt's house. She said the neighbors were there and everyone had cooked and brought food to the house, so people could eat together, and she said the minister was at the house, also. We all finally left the funeral home and went to the aunt's home, and she begged her son in law not to leave this evening and finally, he agreed to stay until early morning, and we were happy he did. We got to talk to the little girl, and she was really sweet, and her dad kept a good eye on her, and got her some food and they sat with us to eat. My mom asked him if he would bring her back to see us, and he said yes. We finally all finished eating and my mom helped the neighbors clean up and put the paper plates in the trash. We were ready to go home. We hugged the little girl and her dad and told them to come see us again and we said bye to the aunt and uncle. They were extremely grieved over the little granddaughter. We left for home, really sad for our mom. She loved her cousin; they were friends growing up and she always talked about how nice she was. We had another exhausting day. My mom got my dad off to work the next morning and she let us stay home again from school but told my older brother he could stay home with us today because we were so tired. My dad came home from work very tired himself, and our mom said she was letting us stay home with our older brother and they would go back to her aunts by themselves today, and we were tired and wanted to stay home, so it was better for all of us. My mom cooked us hot dogs with chili for dinner before they left, and they didn't eat with us because they had to go back with the aunt and uncle and be with them again. My older brother let me help him wash dishes and clean the kitchen up and mom and dad left to the aunt's house. Our older brother turned the radio on and let us listen to music and we liked that. We got the puzzle out and started putting it together again and we were tired and baby brother fell asleep on the sofa and older brother asked if we would want to go to bed and we said yes, so he got baby brother's pajamas and put them on him and he didn't even wake up. We all went to bed and the older brother reminded us that the funeral would be tomorrow and that we would have to go. We don't know when our mom and dad will come home. We were all asleep. My mom didn't wake any of us up until 8 a.m. My dad didn't go to work, so we had to hurry and get ready for the funeral. We had cereal for breakfast, and we quickly got ready to go. My dad had to shine his shoes again and we all wore our best clothes. We drove to the funeral home, and we all had to follow the hearse family directly behind the hearse. We were going to the graveyard, and they had a tent over the grave, and we all got out of our cars and walked to the grave site. The hearse pulled over to the gravesite and sat the coffin on some big belts to be able to lower it down into the grave. Everyone was quiet and the minister came over by the coffin and introduced himself and began to read the eulogy of her life. It was so sad and when it was over, they sang Amazing Grace, and the minister said a prayer, and everyone began walking to their cars and saying goodbye. We were all in the car and my mom was so sad. She looked back toward the grave and said, "I hope God is with her." I asked if we would see her again and she said, "I hope so." My dad was quiet. He didn't like to see anyone cry or be sad.

"LETTER FROM AUNT"

He drove by the post office and had our older brother go in to see if we had mail and he came out with a lot of mail and handed my mom a fat envelope. It was from our aunt in Baltimore. We couldn't wait to see what she had to say. Mom said our older brother could read it to us when we got home. We were soon home, and we all sat down in the living room and our brother began to read the letter to us. She said she was fine but was going to have a baby and mom said, "Oh no, if her husband has to go to jail, it will be worse on her." She asked if we could come to see her in the summer when school is out, and we were hoping for that. Finally, our brother quit reading. It was a long letter and my mom said we could have soup and grilled cheese for dinner, and we were happy, and she quickly made that for us and told us to get ready to go back to school in the morning and we did as she said.

We only had two days of school left for this week and she said we had to go; also, our dad had to go to work. We all were really tired from the sadness and stress of our mom's cousin dying. We all wanted to go to sleep. My dad turned the radio on to listen to the news and the rest of us went to bed; it wasn't quite dark, but we didn't care we were so tired.

We all were up early the next morning, and my mom made us cereal and hot chocolate and she made my dad's lunch for work and ours for school. My mom and dad had coffee and our older brother had hot chocolate with us. We all felt as if another sad chapter had closed in on our lives. It was nice to get to school and see everyone again. There was too much fright and sadness in our lives the past few years. We all needed to be happy and have some peace. It was hard to keep my eyes open at school all day, but the day went by really fast and soon we were on the bus going home. It was a happy day with sunshine and my mom was happy we were home. We set the table because dad would be home soon. Our mom told us to go to the table and we would wait for our dad to come home.

"LETTER FROM BROTHER"

She said he's running late. Finally, he came home. He had stopped by the post office and got our mail. He had a letter and handed it to our mom. It was from our oldest brother; and mom said she would read it to us after dinner and we said OK.

Soon everyone left the table and went to the living room and our mom began to read the letter and he said he would come see us next weekend and take our older brother with him so he could get a good job. I started crying and my brother who went to school with me was crying and our baby brother was crying, because we were crying; and my mom asked us all to stop crying and finally we did. Our older brother told us he would come back on weekends and be with us and that he would always come back and see us; but we still didn't want him to go. We got ourselves ready for bed and our dad turned the radio on to listen to the news and me and my younger brother kept staring at our older brother and my mom told us to go to bed. I heard my mom say to our older brother, "This will be hard for all of us when you leave." He said, "I know." He said good night to mom and dad. I laid awake a long time before I went to sleep thinking how sad it would be when he would leave us. It was hard to imagine, so I asked God to help us get through it and fell asleep.

We all slept in this morning. It was Saturday, and I asked my dad if he would take us to town and let us walk around. It was a warm day and my dad looked at the thermometer on the porch and he said it was sixty-five degrees, and that made me happy because I wanted to see "Gypsy". We loved her and in the winter months she would only come out on warmer days and walk all over. We would have dad stop the car and let us out on the sidewalk, and we would run to her hugging her, and she loved to see us. My dad would park the car and they would come talk to her some and then shop for groceries and let our older brother stay with us while we talked to "Gypsy". My dad would give her a dollar to read his hand and leave us talking to her while they were shopping, and she would always read our hands and tell us good things and make us feel good. Then our dad would drive by and pick us up on the street and we would go home and talk about "Gypsy". We all loved her. The weekend went very fast, and we were back to school Monday morning and dad was back to work. The day at school seemed long and I was worrying about our eldest brother coming to take our older brother away. Finally, the school bell rang, and we all were on the bus going home. We got off the bus and ran up the hill on the dirt road and our older brother was outside. He had chopped up a lot of wood and stacked it by the porch, and I knew he was trying to leave us lots of wood for the stove and fireplaces. He stopped and went into the house with us, and we all washed our hands and helped my mom set the table and was waiting for our dad to come home. He arrived and we all sat down for a large dinner. It was so good that he was working. We had plenty to eat when he wasn't gambling, or drinking. We all finished our dinner and our older brother, and I washed and put away the dishes. My dad was in the living room with the news on the radio and we were quiet and getting ourselves ready for school the next day. My mom said she would be having the baby soon, but none of us were very happy because we all knew our brother would be leaving us soon.

We all were ready for bed after the news went off, so we said good night to each other and went to bed. I was saying my prayers to myself and praying that our oldest brother wouldn't come until the weekend. Finally, I fell asleep.

"THE SADDEST DAY IN OUR LIFE ARRIVED"

We got ready to go to school and my dad went on to work. Time was passing fast, and we were afraid for our older brother to leave us. We finally left and made it to the bus stop. The bus came very quickly, and we were soon in school, and I was worrying all day about our oldest brother coming to take our other brother away. We didn't want that to happen. Our day at school went by fast and we were back on the bus going home. Soon as the bus let us off, we ran up the hill and we saw a new Ford car parked beside the yard and we started running to the house. My brother ran straight to the car and opened the door and sat down in it. I went on into the house, and my eldest brother was talking to my mom and picked me up and said I had grown a lot, and then my younger brother came in and he picked him up and said he had gotten much taller. We were happy to see him, and my younger brother said, "I like your car." My eldest brother said, "I'll take all of you for a ride in it." That made us happy. Our dad walked through the door and asked, "Is that your car?" The eldest brother said, "Yes." Our dad said it was very nice. Our mom and older brother put the food on the table, and we all sat down together. After dinner, my mom said for all of us to go into the living room with our dad and she would take care of the kitchen. We were all happy and our dad was asking our eldest brother about the Korean War, and we were hearing things we had never heard before. It was sad for the children and the separation of families. He said many children became orphans and had to be put in camps, and they were trying to find relatives to take the children. My mom walked in and changed the subject. She asked the eldest brother when they would be leaving, and he said the day after tomorrow because he must get back to work and older brother must get a job. We all were looking sad, and the eldest brother said he would take us for a ride in his new car tomorrow.

My mom told us to get ready for bed and we put our pajamas on, and she let us sit in the living room for a while, and then told us to go to bed. They sat up talking and I don't know when they went to bed.

The next morning, it was Friday, and mom let us stay home from school, but dad went on to work. I asked our eldest brother when he was taking us for a ride in his car, and he said soon as we ate breakfast and got ready, so we were hurrying up so we could ride in his car. Our mom and older brother cleaned the kitchen up quickly and our eldest brother told all of us to go to the car, and we all were happy to get in the car. He drove us all over our small town and bought us ice cream at the drugstore and when we walked out, I saw "Gypsy" and ran straight into her arms and my two younger brothers were hugging her, also. "Gypsy" asked our mom if our eldest brother was the one who was in the Korean War, and my mom said yes. "Gypsy" said he was a gorgeous young man and he smiled and thanked her. "Gypsy" walked with us to the car and told our brother he had a beautiful car, and we hugged her bye, and I told her we would see her again, soon. Our brother asked if we wanted to ride up the mountain and we said yes, so he took us to the top of the mountain and there was a place where cars could pull over and we all got out and looked over the mountain. It was very steep, and the valleys were deep, and we could see two log cabins far down in the valley. It was so far down that they looked very small, and it made you feel a little dizzy when you kept looking down. Our eldest brother suggested we better get back in the car and go home; so, we all got in and going back down the mountain, the curves seemed much steeper than going up because you must brake so much. Our two younger brothers fell asleep and when we got home our mom had to wake them up to get them out of the car. We all went into the house and were happy we got to ride in the new car.

Our eldest brother asked our mom if she would make him home-made chili and hot dogs and she said yes, she would, and that made us all happy. Our dad wouldn't be home from work for three hours. We all went in the living room and sat down, and I looked at my eldest brother and said, "You're leaving Sunday, right?" My mom quickly said, "We don't want to talk about that today." My mom quickly went to the kitchen, and she got the puzzle out and handed it to my older brother and told him and the eldest brother to help younger brother to put the puzzle together. I went back in with all the brothers and got some little cars out for baby brother, and he was happy playing with them. My younger brother who was next to me had become really skilled putting the puzzle together; we had done it so much, it seemed he had memorized the shape of the pieces, and the older brothers were laughing because he was doing better than them. Our mom had begun to make dinner and they were still putting the pieces together and laughing. I walked back into the kitchen with mom, and she said our dad would be home in fifteen minutes. The time passed fast, and they finished the puzzle as our dad walked in the door. We all went to the kitchen to wash our hands and we all seated ourselves and the homemade chili smelled really good. Everyone was passing the dishes around and helping the younger boys make their hot dogs and we all were eating, and I was looking at my dad staring at my two younger brothers, and I knew what he was thinking about them, and how sad they would be tomorrow. We all finished eating and our mom said for me to stay with her in the kitchen and all the boys went into the living room with dad and they were talking. Mom reminded me to not talk about our brothers leaving, and I said OK. We all were tired, and mom got our pajamas, and we stayed up a little longer and then went to bed.

Our mom, dad, and older brothers got up early and that was unusual for Saturday morning. My mom had breakfast cooked and I got up at 6 a.m. to hear them talking. She told me not to wake my brothers up and I said OK and washed my hands and sat down at the table. My eldest brother carried an old suitcase and a shopping bag out to his car. It was then I realized they were going to leave today; and I asked my mom if that was right and she said yes, and for me to be quiet. They all sat down to eat, and tears were running down my cheeks and my brothers said, "Please don't cry, we will come back a lot to see all of you." I got up from the table and went into the room where our younger brother was sleeping and bumped into his bed trying to wake him up. I didn't want to cry alone. We all went to the living room to sit down, and my younger brother got up and walked into the living room and asked why we didn't wake him up. My mom said we let you sleep so you wouldn't be tired, and he looked at our older brother Pippy and said, "You are leaving." He pointed to our eldest brother Herby and said, "You are taking him with you, and we don't want you to do that." Pippy looked at him and said, "I promise we will come back a lot to see you." That's when he started screaming and crying and saying, "You don't love me, if you did, you would stay here." They were hugging us and kissed us on the cheek to tell us bye and I was crying again, and our youngest brother got up and found out they were leaving, and he was screaming. Both older brothers had tears in their eyes and was walking to the car and our dad had to hold on to my younger brother, he was trying to go to the car with them when they pulled away in the car, both of my younger brothers crawled under the bed screaming and crying and I sat down in the living room crying. We felt like we lost everything. Our parents had tears in their eyes and my dad told my mom, "Let the boys stay under the bed crying and they will get tired and come out." I helped my mom in the kitchen, and she took care of the beds, except the one my brothers were under. They were still sniffling and wouldn't talk to us.

I walked out of the house and started looking at the mountains and wondering if I would ever see my brothers again, and tears were falling from my eyes again. I felt so lonely. Families in the mountains were very close and people really loved each other. I walked a short distance out the dirt road and turned back toward the house and my mom and dad were sitting on the swing looking at me and they said the boys had quit crying and had fallen asleep under the bed. They were so tired, so they left them sleeping.

My dad said not to wake them, they needed to rest, and I was happy for them to quit crying. We went back to the house and sat down on the sofa and my mom said she had an appointment with her doctor for a check up on Monday. She said the baby was due in two weeks and I said, "I hope it's a girl. There are too many boys in the family." We heard my brothers making noises coming out from under the bed. Their eyes were swollen underneath them from crying, and they still were not very happy. They were looking out the window where our brother's car had been, and they wouldn't say anything. My dad told us to get ready and he would take us to town and buy us an ice cream at the drugstore; so, we got ready really fast, and we all went to the car. My dad drove us straight to the drugstore and we all went in and sat in a booth and ordered our ice cream. The boys seemed to cheer up some and we left the drugstore, and I asked my dad to drive us by the department stores and let us get out and look in the windows and he did. I was hoping to see "Gypsy", but didn't see her there, so I asked him to drive us by the car lot and we headed that way and drove about a block, and I saw "Gypsy". I was saying, "Stop the car", and he did. We ran up the sidewalk and "Gypsy" sat her shopping bags down and we ran straight into her arms. We were so happy to see each other. We told her our brothers had left together so the younger one could get a job. She told us not to worry; they would come to see us. My dad stuck his hand out for her to read his palm and he gave her a dollar and then she was reading my palm. She always made me happy, and we all loved her. She asked my mom when the baby was due, and my mom said in about two weeks. My dad asked her if she wanted a ride home and she said she loved walking. I don't remember her ever accepting a ride. That was the highlight of our day; and we headed home after hugging "Gyspy". We soon were back home, and my mom made us soup and grilled cheese and we loved that. We were tired after supper, and we all went to bed early.

"SUNDAY MORNING AFTER OUR OLDER BROTHER LEFT"

We all got up a little late and my mom was cooking as usual and none of us was talking much. We were all sad. We finished breakfast and I helped mom and washed the dishes and she put them away. She then got our school clothes together for Monday morning as she always did, and we bathed ourselves and were ready for bed. The day passed fast without any of us talking much. We were just thinking about our lives. Mom got bacon out of the fridge and sliced it and put it back in the refrigerator and I asked if she would make French Toast for dinner with the bacon, and she said yes. We all went to the living room and sat down, and we were all tired and dad turned the radio on, and the boys and I fell asleep, and we woke up about two hours later and mom was making French Toast and bacon. We hadn't had French Toast in a long time, but we really liked it. We all were tired from grieving over our brother leaving. My two younger brothers were sitting on the sofa saying our older brother would never come back, and they were crying, and our mom said they would have to go to bed, and I said I wanted to go to bed because I was tired. We said good night and mom and dad went to bed, too.

"BABY GIRL DAY"

We were off to school early. My baby brother was in second grade already, growing tall. Friday went fast at school, and we were soon off the bus and running up the hill on the dirt road running to the house, and no one was there to greet us. There was a note on the table that the neighbor had taken our mom to the hospital, and she said she would notify our dad at the mines, so he could go to the hospital and stay with our mother. It was very lonely coming home, and no one was there. We didn't lock our doors, unless we were going away. We were home about one hour, and our dad came home and said, "You have a baby sister.", and I was happy for that, but my brothers were hoping for another boy. Our neighbor cooked dinner and brought it to us. She was really kind and we appreciated it. Dad said our mom had to stay in the hospital three days, but he took us to see her and the baby. She was tiny and a pretty baby to take home. We didn't stay long at the hospital, and we all went home. Our neighbor came by and brought us dinner she had cooked again, and it was really good.

We didn't have many dishes, but I washed the dishes and bowls to give back to our neighbor. We all were anxious for mom and the baby girl to come home.

Time passed fast, and mom and baby girl were released from the hospital. She was very tiny. I got to hold her first, then each brother held her, and baby brother was jealous when our dad held her. He started crying and my mom told him we all loved him, and he got to hold the baby again, and he quit crying. Time was passing fast with school, and I wanted it to go faster so I could take care of my little sister.

My dad had stopped by the post office and got a letter from our brothers. They each wrote a full page to us, and we were happy. They said they would come to see us at the weekend, and that made us overjoyed. We didn't even want to go to bed, but we finally did. We woke up early. It was Friday, and our dad had gone to work, and we had a good day. The baby was sleeping mostly all day. Our mom was cooking dinner for us, and she made a long grocery list and said she would make a cake and a lemon pie for us to eat when our brothers came tomorrow. I helped my mom in the kitchen and when our dad came home, we all sat down for dinner and afterward, my mom made dishwater and left me to clean up the kitchen, but they took baby sister with them to the grocery store. I quickly cleaned up the kitchen and we were waiting for them to come home. We turned the radio on, and they came back shortly afterward. They even bought us some cookies and we had cookies and milk before we went to bed. Our mom stayed up and baked the pie and cake for tomorrow. I smelled them baking and fell asleep anxiously waiting for tomorrow.

"BROTHERS COMING HOME"

We all woke up early. It was Saturday morning, and we were all anxious to see the "boys", as our dad called them. We quickly ate breakfast, and I helped mom clean the kitchen and we made the house look good and put on our best clothes and kept asking when they would get here, and my dad said they had to drive all night after getting off from work, so he didn't know. Our baby sister woke up and was making noises and my mom handed me a warm bottle of milk to feed her and baby brother sat beside me as close as he could and asked if he could hold the bottle for her and my mom said for a little while, but he didn't especially like doing that, so he went to sit by our dad. Finally, our baby sister finished her bottle, and our middle brother went out on the front porch and sat on the swing watching for our brothers to come home. He sat there for about an hour, and we heard him jump out of the swing and run to the door and was saying, "They are here!", and he was jumping up and down he was so happy. We all walked out in the yard to greet them. We were all excited and they were too. Our mom said let's go in the house and sit down, and we did. She asked if she could make breakfast for them, but they said they already stopped and ate along the way, so she made them some coffee and gave them some cookies and they wanted to see their baby sister. Mom got her out of the crib and handed her to the older brother first, and he was happy to hold her and then our other brother reached for her, and he held her for a while and mom took her back to her crib. The brothers liked her and said she was a pretty baby. Our oldest brother said we could ride to town, and he would buy us some balloons and candy and we were happy and wanted to go. Mom got everything ready, and we left for town and our older brothers said the town looked so small after they were living in a big city, but they both said they missed the mountains. They took us to the drugstore and bought us all an ice cream and some candy to take home and we were happy. He drove us to the Five and Ten store and bought us some big colorful balloons. When we came out of the Five and Ten, he let the convertible top down and rolled the windows up so mom could sit in the front seat with the baby, so the wind wouldn't bother her. He drove us all over the small town and they were looking at the mountains as if they missed them. We were so happy they came to see us. It was a warm day and we had four big balloons in the car with the top down and that was exciting for us; it was the first convertible we ever rode in, and it was still a new car. We asked our brothers if they had lots of money in their wallets and they said yes. We wanted to see it and they said when we get home.

Our dad suggested we go home because it was cloudy in the mountains, and it may rain; but our brother said he would put the top up if it started to rain. We headed home and we were happy. When we got home, mom headed to the kitchen and baby sister was asleep and she put her in the crib. We all sat down in the living room, and I asked our brothers to let us see their money, and they opened their wallets, and they had a whole lot of twenty-dollar bills, and some fifty-dollar bills. The last time I seen that was when our dad ran the business. We were so happy with our brothers' home, but we knew they would have to go back. We all kept talking, and I walked back into the kitchen with our mom, and she was preparing a great meal for us. Everything was colorful and she baked a big chicken. I couldn't wait to eat the good smelling dinner. I set the table for my mom, and she carved the chicken on a platter and looked like enough meat for two families. She cooked all fresh vegetables. We usually had canned ones, but she felt this dinner was special for us, and made flaky buttered rolls. She finished putting everything on the table and asked me to call all the family to the table and they all quickly washed their hands and sat down. Our older brothers said they hadn't had a meal like that in a long time. We were all happy and enjoying the good food. Finally, everyone was through eating dinner, and we helped her clear the table and she put the leftover chicken and vegetables in the refrigerator, and I helped her clean up all the dishes and our dad was in the living room talking with all the kids. Mom was setting the table for dessert and baby sister had woken up and mom was heating her a bottle and called everyone in for dessert. We had a large lemon pie and a three-layer cake, and mom handed baby sister to me, and the warm bottle and I was feeding her the bottle at the table, and she was quiet. Mom served up the cake and pie to everyone and poured coffee to our older brothers, herself and our dad; and poured milk for us kids and took baby sister from me and held her while she ate her pie and had her coffee. We were all grateful for the great meal she made, and we were happy to be together. We all went back to the living room and our eldest brother motioned to me to come with him to the kitchen and he washed all the dessert dishes, cups and glasses and had me dry them and put them away.

The next morning, our brothers were getting their clothes together and mom handed them a bag with their lunches she made for them, and they were happy and thanked her. She was trying to keep us from crying. Our brothers were ready to go, so we all walked outside with them, and they hugged us and said goodbye, and both younger brothers started crying and trying to hold on to them and they got in the car with them, and dad had to pull them out. They ran into the house crying and crawled under the bed screaming, again. Our brothers didn't get out of the car and as I seen the taillights of the car disappear, I was crying, too. It seemed so permanent to us when they left. We were lonely. We went back into the house and the younger brothers were still under the bed crying. Dad tried to get them out and told mom to leave them alone and they would get tired and come out later, and they did.

It was nearly four p.m., and the younger brothers finally came out from under the bed, and they cried so much their eyes were swollen. Mom was making leftovers from dinner yesterday and we still had some cake and pie for dessert. The baby was crying, and she told the boys to sit on the sofa, she would let them hold the baby and that made them happy at the time. Mom prepared our dinner and asked us to come to the table and she brought the baby to the table with her and had a bottle for her, so I quickly ate and took the baby from her and fed her the bottle. She stayed awake for the next two hours and mom rocked her to sleep and laid her on the sofa and she slept another hour. We were all tired and getting ready for bed and mom made the baby her night bottle and wrapped it in a towel with a hot water bottle to keep it warm. We all went to bed.

The next morning, we all got up a little later than usual, but I heard my mom making the baby a bottle real early, but she went back to bed, and we all got up about ten o'clock, and I asked if we could have cereal for breakfast and mom said yes. I cut some bananas to go in it and she made hot chocolate for us, and we all were happy. We all went to the front porch and sat on the swing and chairs and soon, mom was going back in to clean the kitchen and make the beds and she took the baby in with her. Our dad was talking to us and asking what we wanted to be when we got older. I said, "A doctor", and he said that would cost over a hundred thousand dollars and we couldn't pay for that; it hurt me when he said that, but I didn't say anything. Baby brother said a policeman and dad said he might could do that. The older brother said he wanted to be a lawyer and said it would cost too much, also. Dad picked his paper up and went into the house and we stayed outside looking at the mountains and trying to think our way out until younger brother wanted to go into the house and we went in with him. Dad was reading the paper and mom was sewing younger brother's pants for him. I asked if me and older brother could go see our school friends and mom said, "Maybe tomorrow." We ended the day talking about our family.

"LONELINESS BEGAN TO SET IN WITH US"

We all went through some tragic things together and we hadn't gone to see my mom's father and mother, but our aunt wrote our mom a letter and said our grandfather and grandmother would be moving to Michigan, and mom said we had to go see them this coming week and say bye to them. It seemed like we were losing our family, and they were all going far away. We were more content to stay home since they all left.

We all sat in the living room and mom headed to the kitchen and said she would make her homemade soup and have some noodles she had made already. Our dad was back at work today and both of my little brothers were next to me and were all trying to help our mom with everything, and we were waiting for our dad to get home so we could all eat together. We were running late, and our dad walked in as we were setting the table and we all sat down and when we finished eating, mom mentioned that her mom and dad would be moving to Michigan and we needed to go see them, and dad said, "Let's go this evening." Mom said, "OK. We will clean up the kitchen and we will be ready."

We were soon in the car and on our way. We all loved our grandmother. She was good to everyone and so were our aunts and uncles. Our grandfather never really liked our dad; they never seen things eye to eye. He didn't want my mom married to him because he had children already. Soon we were pulling into the drive of our grandparents' house and our grandmother came to greet us along with the aunts and uncles. We were happy to see each other, and our grandfather said he was going to get a job in an auto plant that was hiring and said that would be good. They all seemed happy to leave the mountains. We stayed with them until it started getting dark and dad said we had to go home, so we hugged all of them goodbye and our grandmother said she would write to us, and we said OK. They told us to come see them and we said we would. They walked out to the car with us, and we left, and our grandmother was tearful, and we were also. My mom said she wished our dad would get out of the coal mines and find a job that wasn't dangerous.

Finally, we arrived home, and we had to get ready for bed because dad had to go to work in the morning. I was so tired I didn't hear mom get up, but she had made breakfast for our dad and took care of the baby's bottle and laid back down and we slept until ten o'clock. We were so tired. We began to count the days until we could go see our brothers on the first of July for two weeks. We helped our mom straighten the house up and I asked her if we could go see our neighbors' children that we went to school with, and she said yes, but we could only stay two hours. We had to be back home before our dad came home and we agreed and mom wrote a note to their mom to send us home at anytime she wished, but we couldn't stay over two hours. We hurried down the hill and into the hollow where they lived, and we were all happy and hugged each other and their mom said our baby brother had grown more than she expected, and he was really cute. He was somewhat shy around other people, but not at home. Our neighbor lady had her children get games out that we could play, and they did. She wanted us inside because she hadn't seen us for a long time. The boys got tired of playing inside and they asked her to go out and she said OK; and I stayed in with her and she had two older girls, and they were talking to me, and we enjoyed each other's company. They had a large family. One girl had already gotten married, and one son was in the service (the Army). They had four sons living at home, and two daughters. One of the daughters made us some popcorn and some Kool-Aid. The boys came back in to have Kool-Aid. We all sat there eating popcorn and drinking Kool-Aid, and a clock was alarming, and the mom said she set the clock for two hours and it was time for us to go home; so, we told them bye.

We hurried home, and my mom asked us if they had asked us anything and I said no. We were all happy to see each other and she said our dad would be home in a little while and she had dinner cooked and had the table set. She told us to wash our hands and we did, and she said to go ahead and seat ourselves at the table. We heard our dad walk through the door and he came in, washed his hands and sat down with us, and said, "You all seem so happy." We said that we were, and mom said she let us go see the neighbors' children and we got to socialize today. We had been through so many bad things it was like we were beat down and scared, and our mom didn't want us to talk about it to anyone, and we wanted to forget it, but you can't erase memories.

We got to sleep late the next morning until nine o'clock, and we were happy. Mom made us cereal and hot chocolate and we loved it. Our baby sister is getting bigger, and she rolls over and tries to crawl. It won't be long until she crawls. She was always quiet and nice. Our mom asked us to put the toys away and we helped her with the baby and made the house look very good. We looked out and the neighbor lady was walking toward the house with the younger children with her; they came up on the porch and their mom was hugging our mom and we were all happy to see each other. Mom made some tea for her, and the neighbor lady and she had Cracker Jack's (small boxes for all of us and they had a little toy inside the box for us to play with). We all were happy and talking. Mom told me to get everyone some milk, but none of us wanted it. We were all happy they visited for a while and then left. We quickly helped our mom clear the kitchen so she could make dinner. Our dad would be home in a short time, and she said she would quickly make us some hot dogs and chili, and we loved that. She finished making it and said in two weeks we would be on vacation, and we would go see our brothers and that made us happy.

Dad just came through the door, and he said, "Hot dogs!" He could smell the chili. Mom told me when I get through eating to take little sister with her bottle in the living room and let her have her milk and she would clean the kitchen up. Finally, mom came into the living room with us and asked dad when we could get new clothes for vacation. He said he would get vacation pay a week before we leave. We were happy to hear that.

We only got new clothes twice a year and the clothes we got for vacation were the clothes we had to wear when school started, and we got clothes for Christmas if they weren't on strike. We didn't have many clothes; we were grateful and took care of what we had. Our mom always polished our leather shoes that we wore in the winter and cleaned our sandals in the summer and tennis shoes. She brush-washed them and hung them on the clothesline to dry. Our clothes were always clean, but we never had many. We all said good night to each other and went to bed.

"WEEK BEFORE VACATION"

Monday morning our dad went to work, and we were talking about getting to buy our vacation clothes Friday. We were anxious the week passed fast, and it was Friday. Our dad took us to town and bought us our dinner at a small restaurant and then we went clothes shopping. We were happy. We all got new shoes and dresses for me, mom and the baby, and the boys got new pants and shirts and dad got new shirts and dress pants. We all were happy with what we got, including new shoes. We left the shoe store and I saw "Gypsy". I ran to her, and my brothers came behind me, and mom and dad walked behind us with the baby in a stroller. "Gypsy" had her arms wide open hugging us and we were all smiling and talking. My brothers loved her just like I did. We were always excited to see her. My dad said he would put the clothes in the car and "Gypsy" could go to the drugstore with us and he would buy us ice cream. We were so happy that she could go with us. We all loved her; she was always kind and sweet and reading our fortune from the palm of our hands made us happy. We all had to go after we ate our ice cream. We hugged her bye and she said she would see us after our vacation, and we went home happy. It was the weekend starting tomorrow and we were all tired and we went to bed anxiously awaiting the next morning.

Saturday morning, I smelled bacon frying. My mom was up earlier than usual. It was eight a.m. and she usually let us sleep later Saturdays, until at least nine a.m., but she was frying the bacon and that usually woke us up. I got up and walked to the kitchen and she had all the plates and silverware on the table. She was happy all of us got new clothes and she wanted to see our brothers as much as we did; and wanted to get out of the mountains and see other places. All the family was up and washing their hands and I put the baby in the highchair. She was now able to eat small spoons of gravy and tiny pieces of biscuits and mom had her a half bottle of milk made, and she took her out of the highchair and put her in the crib and she held her own bottle up now and finished it and sat up in her crib wanting out. Mom put a large blanket by her crib on the floor and sat her on it and she started crawling all over. My dad said she will be walking soon, and mom said that is when she will be a lot of work. I told my mom I would wash the dishes and she could go into the living room with dad and the boys. I hurried up and got the kitchen cleaned up fast and went in with the rest of the family and mom had moved the big blanket to the living room floor and baby sister crawled off it and was trying to pull herself up in a chair but sat back down on the floor. We were all happy to see the progress she had made. My dad walked out on the porch and got his newspaper and sat down in the swing to read it. Mom stayed in the house and was talking to us and telling us we would have to help her get all our clothes and shoes together this week because we would be leaving early next Saturday morning. We were anxious to see our brothers. Our dad came back into the house and said he would take us to see the big rock where history said the rebels drove the Yankees over the big rock and they and their horses died there.

We liked to pick berries and see the Honey Suckle bushes; they were beautiful, and we could see for miles into the valleys. We made it up to the huge rock and picked a bouquet of Honey Suckle flowers for our mom. They were bright orange and beautiful, and we picked some blueberries and put them in a bag, and we were getting tired. Our mom had made us some Kool-Aid in a big jar with ice in it and we had paper cups to drink out of and it tasted very good. We were hot and thirsty and ready to go home. Dad told us to get in the car so we could go home, and we did. Our dad was driving slow down the mountain; it was very steep and curvy. We were all anxious to get home. Mom said she would make homemade vegetable soup and grilled cheese and we all liked that. We had a half gallon of blueberries for dessert, and we all liked them. We were happy to get back home and have our dinner over with. We felt like we had a great day, and we were discussing our trip to go see our brothers. We were all tired and went to bed.

The next morning, we all got up happy and we ate breakfast and cleaned everything up fast and our mom said we could all begin to get our clothes ready to go see our brothers. We didn't have many clothes, but we had enough. We helped her put everything we wanted in the empty corner, and she got the only suitcase she had, and some suit bags to hang clothes on hangers and a big shopping bag to put our dress shoes in. We had everything set to go and she said we could pack everything tomorrow and leave Saturday, and we were happy to hear that. We got up early the next day and we quickly got our clothes together and had a check-off list, so we wouldn't forget anything. Our dad said he would place everything in the trunk of the car today because we would have to leave at four a.m. in the morning and we would not be eating that early; but our mom would make the baby a bottle of milk and that would keep her quiet. Our mom quickly made us French Toast, bacon and cocoa, and we really liked that. She had a lot of French Toast left over and said we could eat it for lunch because she had to use the bread and eggs up before, we left, but that me us happy because we would have cocoa again.

I asked our dad if he would take us to town later this evening and he said yes, if we wanted to go, but we would have to hurry home and go to bed early and we said we would. Time seemed to go fast today. We had finished off the French Toast at twelve o'clock and our dad said he would take us to town at four o'clock and we happily ran to the car and was on our way. He drove us straight to the drugstore and bought us soup and a sandwich and after we ate that we got to have ice cream. We were all happy after we left the drugstore. We were walking around, and I saw

"Gypsy" and I started running to her and hugging her, and my brothers were hugging her, too. We all loved her. She asked where we had been and we told her we were going to see our brothers and she said she would love to see them, also. We kept talking to "Gypsy" and our dad said we must go home, and we had to tell her bye and we had tears in our eyes and "Gypsy" said, "When you come back; come and see me." I said that we would and headed for the car and when we got in my dad looked at me and said, "I knew why you wanted to go to town." I said, "You are right." He laughed and drove us home, and mom said get ready for bed. You all know we must leave early, so we did as she said.

"LEAVING TO SEE FAMILY"

The next thing I knew, she was waking us up at four a.m. and we were happy. We got ready fast as we could, and mom made the baby a bottle and we were on our way to see our brothers!

It was still dark when we left, but slowly began to break daylight. My baby sister and younger brother were sleeping, and mom said let them sleep or they will all be tired and cranky, so we stayed quiet. Finally, I looked over at my older brother and his head was nodding and he went to sleep, and it was catching because I couldn't hold my eyes open any longer and I was asleep, too.

Next thing I heard was baby sister crying and we all woke up. Dad was pulling into a gas station and mom got a diaper for the baby. She said she wet her diaper, and she changed her, and she quit crying. Dad told us if we had to use the restroom for mom to take me with her and when we came back, he would take the two boys. That way the baby would be in the car with someone while he pumped gas. Finally, we were back in the car and mom asked dad if the boys washed their hands and he said yes. Our mom was very strict about hand washing. Dad said he asked the man at the gas station where a good restaurant was for breakfast, and he told him a mile up the road the same way we were going. He said it had a red front and sure enough we saw a restaurant with a red front and our dad pulled the car up close to it. We all got out and I asked my mom what time it was, and she told me it was eight thirty in the morning and I was looking around and didn't see any mountains. It looked like the sky was touching the ground. We went on in the restaurant and my mom said, "Look how clean it is in here", and she said, "I hope the coffee is good." The waitress seated us and got a highchair for the baby, and we were all ordering our breakfast. Mom and dad had coffee and they ordered us cocoa to drink, and we had eggs and bacon and homemade biscuits. Everything was really good. Mom fed my baby sister a scrambled egg and some applesauce. She really loved it. We all finished up and got back in the car and were on our way again. I asked our dad how much longer it would be to where our brothers lived, and he said about three and a half hours. That seemed like a long time, and we were very anxious. We passed through several small towns and lots of big farms and many of them had horses.

Our mom asked our dad if he was tired of driving and he said, "Yes, but no one else can help me drive." Our mom never got her driver's license. She was like most of the women in Appalachia, they didn't want a driver's license. They all seemed subservient to their husbands in Appalachia. The men worked very hard in the coal mines and the women kept house and worked in the vegetable gardens and canned their food from the gardens in the fall. They also had quilting parties in the winter. Most of the time there were about six women working on a quilt. They would buy material and supplies, and they would start with one quilt at a time and wouldn't stop until they made six quilts, and each woman would make her own quilt. When they had finished, some of them were really beautiful.

"SEEING OUR BROTHERS"

My mind wondered off to how people really lived in Appalachia and my dad had kept driving and we were all getting tired and he said he was going to stop at the next gas station and we could have a cold pop while he pumped the gas and we all went to the bathroom and washed our hands; when we got back in the car, our dad said we are about forty five minutes from our brother's house and that really woke us up. Finally, we were pulling into the driveway at a small white house with flowers around the porch. It was really neat. We went up the steps and knocked on the door and both brothers told us to come in and we went in, and we were all hugging each other. It was a great moment in time. We were with them. They had one of their girlfriends make dinner for us, and she cooked very well. We all were introduced to her, and we thanked her for cooking for us, and she said she had to go home for the night. We told her to come back and see us and she said she would. Our brothers told us they would take us to an amusement park tomorrow, so we could have fun and ride the Ferris wheel and the merry go round, and that made us happy. Our brothers said we could take a shower tonight so we could hurry when we got up and get ready in the morning. Our mom got our night clothes out for us and told us to sit down by the bathroom door until she got some towels and wash clothes, and soap for us and she said I could get in the shower first, and she would help me, and wash my back. I had never had a shower before and I really liked it, and didn't want to get out, but I knew my brothers would like it, also. Mom helped me out of the tub and dried my back and handed me my little night gown, and I put it on, and she put both my brothers in the shower together and they were laughing and soon she had our brothers in their pajamas, and she put them in the bed together and she closed the doors of the rooms we were in, and they stayed up talking.

We woke up the next morning and mom was in their kitchen making breakfast for us all, and we washed our hands, and she seated us at the table and our brothers seated themselves at the kitchen counter and mom gave them plates, forks, and a spoon and everyone was eating and anxious to go to the amusement center. Finally, all of us were ready and we rode in the car with our brothers and mom, dad and baby sister followed us in their car. Our brothers drove us into another town and stopped at our aunt's house. She lived in the town where the amusement park was located, and we were all happy to see each other and our other brother who lived with her was invited to go with us, and we were really happy.

We visited with our aunt for about two hours and had ice cream and cake with them and went on to the amusement park. We were so happy to have our other brother with us and he was, too. Our dad said his sister told him to have us back there at six p.m., and she would have a big dinner made for us, and she was a good cook, and owned a grocery store, so she always had plenty of food.

"THE AMUSEMENT PARK"

Our older brothers told us to look ahead after several minutes had passed and we seen a huge Ferris wheel in the air, and we were very excited to see that, and I asked if I could roll the window down and point out the Ferris wheel to mom and dad who were following behind us and he said yes. I put my arm out the window and pointed ahead to the giant Ferris wheel in the air and our dad honked the horn and we knew he had seen it. Our brother who was driving the car turned on the street near the giant Ferris wheel and he stopped at a small building and paid a man some money for parking and also paid for our dad's car to park, and we all were getting out of the car and walking into the park where all the rides were and our dad handed our brothers money to pay for our rides and they wouldn't take it. They said they wanted to pay for everything for us to ride and that was their treat to us. We headed for the Ferris wheel, and older brother got on with me, and younger brother, and middle brother got on with our brother that lived with our aunt, and we were soon having the time of our life. We were somewhat scared when we were on top and it headed down, but we got used to it and liked it. It was much bigger than the ones we rode at the carnival in the mountains, and we could see all the rides from up high. It looked like a city of different things to ride, and when we got off, we headed for the merry go round, and the horses on it were really beautiful white, black, brown, and beautiful trim on them. We just loved it! When we got off that ride, our dad had bought us a Coke and popcorn and we quickly ate the popcorn and drank the Coke. Then, our brothers took us to the bumper cars where we stopped ourselves and bumped into each other. That was a lot of fun.

After the bumper cars, our brothers took us to a place where we could win things and they had to throw the balls. We were too short and not strong enough to throw the balls, so they did it. They won some little cars and a bow and arrow, which they divided amount the boys and our dad said he wanted to throw the balls to win something, and he knocked down three things and he won a huge doll with a long dress and mom said I could keep it on my bed, and I really like it. We kept walking and they stopped at a stand where they had large hoops to throw over things and if the hoops went on the little sticks standing up, you won a prize, and they won a beaded necklace for me, and I was happy. We walked all over the park and baby sister was in a little stroller and mom put a pillow on the tray of the stroller and she had her head on it and was sleeping. We all were getting tired, and the sun was heading down, and dad said we needed to go back to his sister's and not be late. Our brothers asked us if we were ready to go and we said yes. We walked all over the park, and it was colorful and beautiful, and we were tired.

We all headed back to the car and mom told us to thank our brothers for the good time we had, and they wanted us to have a good time, and we did. We walked back to the car and got in and fell asleep, we were so tired.

"AUNT'S FOR DINNER"

We woke up when they pulled into the aunt's drive and we all got out and my older brothers went in with us, and the first thing I seen was a beautiful set table with China and crystal and the house and furniture was very nice. Mom had us go to the bathroom to wash our hands and we then sat down at the large table. It seated twelve people, and our aunt came in serving the food and everything looked perfect.

We had the most fun and happiness we ever had, and we didn't want to go back to the mountains; so many bad things happened to us there. We could not wipe all the bad things from our minds. It was like a nightmare that never ended.

We all thanked our aunt for the good dinner we had, and dad told his sister we had to leave because we are staying all night with our brothers, and we will be going home by noon tomorrow. We arrived back to where our brothers lived, and mom said we had to take a bath because we would be on the road all day tomorrow. Our brothers said they only had a shower, and I was happy to hear that because I hated those number two wash tubs. We took our showers quickly and put our pajamas on and headed to bed. We were tired. Mom and dad stayed up with our older brothers talking with them, and we were tired and went to sleep.

We all got up the next morning and dad said he would take us to breakfast, and we were happy to hear that, and we got ready fast. Our brothers said they would direct us to their favorite breakfast bar, and it was a big, crowded breakfast place, and we were ordering breakfasts with everything and pancakes. It was a good place to eat, and we enjoyed it.

We all walked out together, and dad had already packed the car and he told us to say bye to our brothers and we did, and we all had a few tears and dad told us all to get in the car and we hugged our brothers and hurried to the car crying. Mom and dad hugged them and got in the car, and we all were waving, and we slowly pulled away. We had a lot of hours before we would get into the mountains. It was very scenic driving through Lexington, Kentucky, and seeing all the beautiful racehorses on the farmlands. Little brother and sister were sleeping, and it was peaceful.

Mom said it was peaceful with them sleeping but we would have to stop and get gas within the hour, and we could use the bathroom when we stopped. Dad said we had about five hours before we would get home, and it would be dark. We were all tired and feeling lonely after seeing our family. I was so tired from talking to everyone and I was getting sleepy myself, and baby sister was waking up and I checked her diaper, and it was wet. We were entering a small town and dad seen a gas station and he stopped there.

He pulled in and told mom to take us to the bathroom and we all got out and stretched our legs and I got in the car and changed little sister's diaper and washed her up. She was never any trouble. Mom bought us some cookies and chocolate milk cartons and we ate the cookies and drank all the milk. Our little sister had her bottle of milk. We were all happy at the time.

The sun was beginning to go down and dad said we would be home in two hours. That sounded good. Mom said our brother told her he had been dating a pretty nice girl and that he may marry her; but he would bring her home to meet us first. We were listening but didn't want to think about it. It got dark really fast. We were in the low hills of the mountains, and we would soon cross one of the big ones. The younger ones were all asleep. My younger brother and sister didn't wake up until we were home. We were really tired. It seemed like a long time coming back. We were all anxious to go to bed. We finally pulled into our driveway, and we went in and got our pajamas on, and mom fixed baby girl's bottle and we all went to bed.

We all slept in until about noon. We were so tired, but mom got up and made baby sister a bottle and she went back to bed, and we all were so tired we didn't feel like getting up. Finally, I heard mom and dad get up; and dad had the radio on for the news and mom was in the kitchen making breakfast. One by one we were getting up and baby sister was cooing now, and she was a happy baby, and I took her into the living room and put her on the sofa with a pillow in front of her and I went into the kitchen to put the plates and silverware on the table. I told dad and my brothers to wash their hands and come to the table. We all were seated, and we began looking at each other. We began to be lonely and missing our aunt and our brothers. They did so much for us, and we went through so many bad things we could never forget them. They stayed in our minds. It has been very hard to write this, and I have cried many tears while doing so. I hope that whoever reads this will see all the sorrow that drinking and gambling can cause and never put their children through this. It was like we had to handle these people and help them, and we were children, and we were learning fast how to cope with it.

It seems like our mom got the brunt of all the bad things that had happened, and it was not her fault, but these things made her nerves really bad, and she had no patience with us kids. We tried to help her all we could, and our baby sister was not a crybaby. She was really good, and we were happy she was a good baby.

We will be going back to school in seven weeks. We were happy to hear that. We were anxious to go back and be happy to see our friends and teachers. There will be no obligations with them. We continued to feel lost with our aunt and brother gone. We had more anxiety, and we were missing them because they looked out for us, and we looked out for them many times. We missed being in the business because we listened to the jukebox and danced with them when we could. It was like our whole world changed and we couldn't talk about it. Mom told dad to get the extended check from his work so we could get school clothes and he did, so we got to go to town to buy some school clothes and we were happy for the moment. We were counting the days for school to start. We had three more days until we could see everyone.

We were happy the miners were back at work, but when they went on strike, we all suffered. We asked dad to take us to town on Saturday so we could talk to all the people. He took us and it was really crowded. They were all school shopping, but we got a parking spot in front of the drugstore and that was good. We could get an ice cream and that made us happy. We all got out of the car, and everyone was talking to us, and mom suggested we go in and sit in the booths and eat our ice cream, so we did. We came back out and people were all over the sidewalks talking with us. They hadn't seen us for a while, and they said baby brother had grown a lot and baby sister was introduced to them. We had a good time talking with them, but it was hot outside and we wanted to go home, so we all walked back to the car and thanked mom and dad for the ice cream and went home.

"LONELY HOUSE"

We all made it fast to the house and we were tired and looking at each other as if we were scared; we did that a lot and I knew what they were thinking about, the place burning and we would have all died, if the competition had not woken us up. None of us will ever forget that; it was a scar in our minds, and we all knew it was a close call. We were kids and sometimes we missed the jukebox and dancing and the slot machines. We didn't understand that it was illegal. We liked to see the people dancing and they liked us.

While I was reminiscing, mom made us grilled cheese, soup, and a salad, and we were happy with that. We were never out of food when they ran the businesses and we didn't have to starve, so we thought that was good. All we can do is pray that everyday will get better for us and that our family will come and see us more. Mom told us to get ready for bed and tomorrow we can get our school stuff together and lay our clothes out for school and take our baths in the evening. We all listened to her and went to bed. I heard her washing the dishes and then I heard dad turn the radio off and they went to bed.

The next morning at seven a.m., I heard mom making baby sister a bottle and she went back to bed. We finally got up at ten thirty. Today was an exciting day for us. We got all our clothes laid out for school and we were excited to see who our teachers would be; younger brother said, "I can start school next year." Mom said, "You are right.", and smiled at him. He never liked being left out. He was very active but nice. We asked mom if we could just have cereal for breakfast and she said OK. I made us all a bowl of Cheerios. None of us were too hungry because we ate late last night. We were getting anxious to go back to school and we asked if we could take our baths early and she said yes; and we did that right away. Dad went up to the little gas station with a small restaurant in it and bought hot dogs and French fries for us. I think they planned to do that because we were thinking back so much.

"GOOD DAY FOR US STARTING SCHOOL AGAIN"

Dad went to work early, and we could smell cocoa and we were happy. We had scrambled eggs and potatoes and we loved that. We were eating really fast so we could get dressed. We couldn't wait to see what teachers we would have. We finished our food and started getting dressed. We were happy and, in a hurry, to get to the school bus stop. We hugged our mom and said bye to her, and we ran all the way to the bus stop. We got there first but seen our friends and neighbors running, also. We all were happy to see each other. The bus driver was a little late, but he was happy and whistling. It seemed like he flew us up there. We were getting off the bus and when we got inside the teachers were dividing us into classes; one of them we knew, and she introduced the new one to us. The new one was teaching the younger children. They both were nice. I was so happy nobody was asking us questions and we were happy about that.

The teachers had many boxes of new books and were letting us pass them out and we were to put our name inside the cover with lead pencils. We were all soon through with that and everyone had their books. The school had only two big rooms and each teacher had all the students seated. They each gave us small assignments and the day passed really fast, but we were happy to be with people we know. The teacher of my class told us to get our books ready to take home and we did and when we were leaving, I could see the other teacher had her student's assigned homework, also.

The bus driver was waiting for us to get on and we all ran to the bus. He didn't waste any time getting us home and we liked that. We were home about thirty minutes and dad's car came down the dirt road and we didn't know he would be home early every day because he was going to work thirty minutes earlier. We won't see him in the mornings because we won't be up when he leaves.

"DINNERS WILL BE EARLIER WITH DAD COMING HOME EARLIER"

It's going to take a while getting to know a few new kids at school and falling back into the teachers' routines. We were staying busy. The teachers gave us a lot of homework to do from Monday through Thursday, but not on Fridays. They wanted us to enjoy our weekends and we liked that. Dad came into the house, and we all got to eat early, and we liked that. Mom said baby sister wasn't feeling good and she would take her to the doctor tomorrow if she wasn't any better. She told us not to get in her face and we didn't. She said it may be the flu. She had never been sick. She told us she will take her to the doctor in the morning if she is not better. She said she will get the neighbor to drive her there. Mom never got a driver's license; she was too nervous to take the test. We took our baths early and got to bed. We got up rested the next morning. We had some fried bologna and gravy and biscuits. It was good. It was a delight to have that. Our day was really good. We went to school, and everything was good.

Mom said she would leave our door unlocked when she took baby sister to the doctor. We went on to school and the day passed fast and before we knew it, we were lining up for the school bus and we didn't have to worry. The driver hurried us home. The door was unlocked, and our dad should be home soon. He saw the neighbor that had taken mom to the doctor's office. She pulled over and dad got mom and baby sister out of her car and thanked her, and they came on up to the house. We were happy to see them. Mom said the doctor gave baby sister an injection and she had two prescriptions for her to get from the drugstore tomorrow, and the doctor said if she's not better in three days to bring her back. Mom changed her diaper and bathed her and gave her a warm bottle of milk and she went to sleep.

Mom told me to get the canned chili out and open it and she got hot dogs out of the freezer and boiled them, and we had canned green beans and hot dogs with chili, and we were happy. Mom told us we could wash ourselves in the wash pan and we could take our baths tomorrow. We liked that and I helped baby brother wash himself and we heard baby sister crying so mom sat her up in a soft chair in the living room and gave her a little red ball to play with and she was quiet. Mom said she would have to keep her up until ten o'clock or she wouldn't sleep all night. My brother had a little schoolwork to do but I didn't have any yet. Dad turned his radio on the news and that always made us kids want to go to bed. We have been playing on the school grounds at school and we run a lot and that makes us go to sleep earlier. We kids all decided to go to bed earlier, and we left mom, dad and baby up. I don't know when they came to bed, I was tired.

Dad got a letter from both our brothers and our brother who went through everything with us is bringing his girlfriend with him to introduce her to us. He said he may marry her.

"PRESCRIPTION DAY!"

Dad had already left for work, so we didn't see him as usual and mom made us eggs and toast and cocoa to drink, we were happy. We have our friends again and we are anxious to go to school. I feel sorry for mom because she stays home a lot and takes care of little brother and baby sister and washes and irons clothes and keeps the house clean. She used to have neighbor friends, but she doesn't want to talk about our lives and what happened and about the constable or the sheriff and the arrest and court room and doesn't want us to say anything, so we must not say anything. We had a good day at school and my brother got a good grade on his homework. We like our teachers and my brother got to ring the bell for us to go home today; and we hurried out to the school bus and the bus driver hurried us home again. We all liked him for that. We got off the bus and ran down the dirt road to the house and dad was sitting in the swing on the front porch. It had been very warm for several days. It was late August. Mom handed dad the two prescriptions and told him to go get them for baby sister and he left to the drugstore, and I started helping mom in the kitchen. I set the table and she said we could eat now.

"HORRIFIC ALMOST DARK"

Mom said she would do the dishes and I asked if I could take baby girl and sit her on my lap in the swing and she said OK, but not for long. I walked out carrying baby girl to the swing and seen dad's wallet in the swing and hurried back and handed it to mom and she said, "I will have to take his wallet and walk down toward town and hope he turns and will see me." The sun was going down and it might have gotten dark. She walked past the Juke Joint, and she said loud music was playing and shortly after that she heard loud footsteps behind her and could see it was a tall man running after her and she started running from him. There was a man her and dad knew who lived there with his wife, and they were at the bottom of the highway and had steps going up to his sidewalk and she was screaming and trying to get up the steps and she fell on the steps and broke her lower false teeth and was still screaming and had cut her knee and the big man landed on her back and put his hand over her mouth and was smothering her and telling her, "If you scream again, I will cut your throat!" She said he had smothered her down and she was praying to God to let her scream again, and she recognized that he was a colored man. That's what they were called then. Finally, she got his hand off of her mouth and gave a loud scream and tried to pull his hair, but her hand slipped off his head. He said, "You scream, and I will cut your throat." She screamed again and the man who lived there came out on the porch and turned the light on and said, "What's going on out there?" The colored man jumped up and ran back toward the beer joint and the man called the constable, and he asked my mom what happened, and she told him he was trying to rape her but couldn't get her skirt up (pencil skirt). The constable drove mom home and dad was there. The pharmacist let him have the prescriptions and said he could pay tomorrow. Me and my brother were so scared to see the blood run down her leg, and she had her teeth in her hand and was very frightened and shaking and dad didn't know what to think. Baby brother started crying seeing the blood. Dad was really white in the face, and he was shocked. Three of her blouse buttons were torn off and she looked like she was in a panic. I felt so bad for her. The Constable told dad he walked her back in the juke joint and had his gun out and told her to look at all the men and see if she can recognize him and she said no; so, he brought her home. It was like she was terrorized; I don't think she could ever forget it. She told me before she died, she forgave him because she wanted to be right with God.

"SCARED ALL THE TIME AND LIVING WITH HORROR"

This bad thing that happened to her changed her so much; we had to keep the doors locked all the time and she told the neighbor boys that came to see us that they must identify themselves when they knock on the door, and they told her they would do that. They seen that she was nervous, but they didn't know what happened and she told me not to tell anyone about it. I said OK.

I had already fixed dad and the boys some canned soup and egg sandwiches and I made baby girl a bottle of milk and she was ready to go to sleep. I asked mom what she wanted to eat, and she said, "Nothing." I finally got her to drink a glass of milk and I made her grilled cheese; she had a very difficult time trying to eat the grilled cheese, but she ate it. I washed my little brother up a bit and put him to bed. My other brother put his pajamas on, and he was snoring soon as he laid down. I stayed up and helped my mom to wash herself up and she told me to get her housecoat and she would put it on and get her night gown and put it on.

I bandaged her leg and her skirt had stuff from him on it! She asked me to get her a shopping bag out of the cabinet and give it to her and I did, and she put all the clothes she had on in the bag and asked me to go outside with her while she burned them, and I did. She was still shaking and crying, and I tried to comfort her, and everyone was in bed but us, so I left her dishes in the dish pan, and I walked with her, and she got in the bed. I kissed her on the cheek and told her good night and she was still shaking.

I got up when mom did and made dad's lunch for him and mom scrambled eggs and fried potatoes and dad quickly ate and hurried off to work. I don't think my brothers understood what happened to her; dad told them somebody was fighting her, but she would be OK. They were looking at her scared. Baby sister was saying mama and dada now and she was always happy.

My brother and I were getting ready for school, and I poured mom a cup of coffee and handed her a plate with eggs and potatoes and toast, and she began crying saying, "I have to get some lower false teeth. I had them since I worked in that factory in Baltimore, my teeth decayed and the other women that worked there said all of them had the same thing happen to them and they had to get false teeth." Nobody knew what caused that. They were making war materials in the factory, but nobody could question it.

My brother and I went to school but all day I was thinking about my mom and how scared she was. She told me not to say anything about it. It seemed like we had only a half a day of school, it went so fast. I was scared to go home the way mom was feeling but I knew we would have to comfort her; and help her get through this. We were frightened for her but didn't say it in front of her. We ran home when we got off the bus. We saw our dad's car and knew he was home and younger brother was on the porch waiting for us.

We went into the house and mom still had that scary look on her face and we hugged her and told her we loved her, and dad was talking to her and told her we will help you get through this, and she nodded her head, yes.

"FIRST WEEKEND OFF FROM SCHOOL"

We didn't have to get up early. Mom had made baby sister her bottle and she was fine. We all got up about nine thirty and quickly had breakfast and we asked if they would take us to town and let us walk around and they said yes, and we were happy. I was praying that we would see "Gypsy" and my prayer was answered and dad pulled the car over and parked and we ran straight to her on the sidewalk, and it was like a family reunion. We were so happy! "Gypsy" hugged baby sister and she was so happy, and she said we were all growing fast and that she loved us all! Dad asked "Gypsy" if she wanted to go to the drugstore with us and he would buy her a chili dog and a milkshake, and she said yes!

We were ecstatic because dad had money at the time, and we weren't starving. We sat there in the drugstore booth, and we finished all our food, and she held our hand one at a time, me and my brother, and as usual, she told me I would have lots of money when I got older and told all of us kids that she just wanted us to be happy. It was a great day in our life just seeing her. We all walked out of the drugstore, and everyone started talking to us and we walked around with "Gypsy" with us for about one hour and "Gypsy" talked to everyone with us, and everyone loved her, also. We soon left and "Gypsy" walked to the car with us, and we all said we were happy we had seen her, and we loved her. We had a great day and we loved it!

On the way home mom told me not to set my heart on what "Gypsy" tells me. She said she wants to make you happy. I said I knew, but she means well, and my brother said we still love her, and mom said we all do.

Dad said our brother Pippy who went through so much with us will be coming to see us and introduce his girlfriend that he might marry. I said I hope he comes, but my older brother with us said he hopes he comes and leaves her home! Mom said don't be jealous!

We were all tired from walking and mom wanted to wash the clothes we had on when we went to town and some more that was in the laundry bag. She got some hamburger patties out of the freezer and put them in a large iron skillet and put a little water in it and a lid on the skillet and turned it on low and told me to watch it; and she had some leftover vegetable soup and she said we could have it with our hamburgers and we all loved that together. I kept watching the food and mom let us put our pajamas on and she washed all the clothes and dad had his news on the radio. My baby sister and younger brother were taking a nap on each end of the sofa and mom said leave them alone. My other brother was reading a comic book that was entertainment in those days. Soon, the water dried up in the skillet and the burgers were frying and mom was hanging the clothes on a clothesline on the porch. She told me to take the burgers up and put the condiments on them and pour the soup in soup bowls. I had everything put together and the older brother woke baby sister and brother up and they had rested good, and everyone was washing their hands and ready to eat dinner.

Mom really looked tired. She said every little noise scared her at night and she was sleeping poorly from being scared. I washed the dishes up and told mom to go listen to the news with dad. I think she was happy to go sit down. It was a good day and a good evening for all of us.

Mom suggested we go turn our spreads on our beds back and we did, and she said go to bed when you want to and I was really tired and I was the first one to go to bed, and that was unusual. I don't know when the others went to bed. The last thing I heard was mom putting baby sister in her crib.

Sunday morning, I heard mom up, so I got up and she was ironing the clothes she had washed and getting things ready for us to go to school. I asked her if we could have French Toast and cereal and she said that would be fine. She seemed to be happy with my suggestions. It was like she was fearful most of the time. That terrible incident was horrific for her, and her doctor told her it will take a long time to get over this. We tried to make life easy on her as best as we could. She told me and my older brother not to talk about this to anyone, and we said OK.

We were doing good in school and liked our teachers. We are hoping our older brother will come next weekend. We will wait and see.

It is Monday, and we are going back to school this morning and trying to be happy. My teacher asked me if my mom was doing OK and I said yes; and I wondered if she had heard something, so I never said anything else. We felt like people had found out the way they were asking questions, but we weren't sure.

We are always tired on Mondays after we go to town and socialize with all the people, but we love to see them, and everyone is nice and well mannered. Some of them bring their dogs with them, but they don't allow them to take the dogs in the stores, but people volunteer to hold on to each other's dog if they want to go in the store. People were genuine in these days, and they helped each other, and most people were happy. We all took our baths earlier than usual so we could go to bed. The weather had been unusually warm for fall, but it is supposed to change this week, but we are ready for it to change. We love to see the leaves falling. They are so beautifully colored, and we liked them. We are looking forward to our brother coming this weekend and getting to see and talk with his girlfriend. We haven't had a lot of company since this bad thing happened to mom. The neighbor kids come and see us and that makes us happy. Mom is afraid we will talk to someone about it, but we don't. We want to forget it, but we can't. It makes you think of a bad car accident where someone got injured badly and it's only about a mile from our house and we must pass it each time we go to town. I asked dad if we could move to town and he said, maybe. I wanted to move to town before I got to high school, and I could have more friends near me, and my brother wanted that too. We had to do what our parent's thought was best for all of us.

We also had to think about the mining strikes and how much rent we would have to pay. The strikes always held everyone back and left them broke; they were very unhappy times and scared us about our livelihood. It sometimes lasted months and that's when many people starved; everyone ran out of food, and they would trade chicken for beef until we had nothing and that's when we only had gravy and bread for breakfast and pinto beans and cornbread for dinner. Sometimes we could buy milk from neighbors but not for long. Some people ate plantains, a green that kept growing, even in the winter. We mixed it with beans, and it was OK.

I will never forget when we had no money and needed food. The small amount the union gave the miners was not enough to feed a family but somehow the God of Heaven brought us through many times.

We all needed the bad things removed from our memory of the

heat from the slot machines and the coolers were bad and the smell was breathtaking. We were devastated.

The week went by very fast and tomorrow will be Saturday and our brother will be here soon. We had our dinner, and we took our baths early and got into bed early so we could get up early before our brother arrived. We were all anxious to see him. Mom and dad went to the living room to listen to the news, and we went to sleep.

"PIPPY IS HERE!"

We all got up early and put on our best clothes. Mom had the house really clean, and we made the beds and made eggs and sausage gravy. We hurried up eating and I helped mom clean up the kitchen. We all went into the living room waiting for our company. About forty-five minutes later, we seen his new car coming toward us on the dirt road and he was blowing his horn, and we were so happy! We walked out on the grass beside the car when he stopped, and younger brother and middle brother were hanging on to him and he was trying to get around the other side to let his girlfriend out; so, I just went around and opened the door for her and introduced myself to her. She was very nice and had a beautiful dress on and her hair was auburn colored and very pretty. We all went into the house and kept talking and the middle brother was keeping an eye on the girlfriend and our older brother was laughing at him. The girlfriend was very pretty, and we all took a liking to her; and middle brother told her he talked to a girl that older brother knew before he left home and she said she would come and see our older brother this weekend and his girlfriend said, "If she comes, I will pull her hair out!" We were surprised that she had a bad temper like that. My mom changed the subject and asked them if they would like baked chicken with stuffing and they said yes. Mom asked the girl if she would mind sleeping with me on a folding bed and she said that would be fine. We already seen she had a temper and mom wasn't sure what she would say, but she was nice about that, and big brother said they would be married in two weeks and middle brother's eyes opened when he heard that.

Mom went into the kitchen and stuffed the chicken and made a large salad and chopped fresh vegetables to cook later and said she would have to cook the chicken slow in the oven. My middle brother whispered to me and said, "She is really pretty." I said, "Yes, she is." Mom asked middle brother if he would watch to see if that other girl was coming to the house and he said he would, and she said to tell her that he is getting married in two weeks; so, don't come to see him. He said, "OK, I will."

Mom asked the girl if she would like to see our small town in the mountains and she said yes. We rode to town in my brother's new car, and it was nice. He drove us all over and the girl said she loved the mountains but didn't like the small town. Dad asked our brother if he would drive us to the drugstore and he said Ok, and dad bought all of us a big ice cream and we sat in the booth and ate it. We were happy to see the girl he is getting married to, and we all liked her very much.

We all left the drugstore and headed home. Mom left the chicken in the oven roasting on low, and all the vegetables were cut up already so there wasn't much to do. We finally made it home and I could smell rosemary and other spices on the chicken, and it smelled really good. She turned the oven up and said the chicken would be done in thirty minutes and she had the vegetables in pots to cook already. I had to ask the girl's name again and she said Mary. Mom told her she could get the rolls out and butter them and put them in the oven in ten minutes, and she got them out and dad and the boys were in the living room talking and baby sister was saying a few words and being good. I set the table, and all the vegetables were done, and the chicken was done. It browned well and Mary put the rolls in the oven and mom asked for everyone to come in and wash their hands and get to the table, and we were all seated, but Mary and mom and they were putting everything on the table, and we all seemed happy about it.

Mary asked if she could say a prayer for the food and we said yes. We were happy she said that. We began respecting her. We usually said prayers at night when we were in bed. Everyone really loved the dinner and mom had Mary cut the big chocolate cake she got for dessert, and we all loved it; baby sister had it all over her mouth and I got a washcloth and washed her face. We all were happy, and it seemed like a day that could last forever.

Mom said she would clean up the kitchen and I told mom I would help her, and older brother, dad, and Mary went in the living room and the kids went with them. Mom quickly washed the table and rearranged the chairs, and we went into the living room with them.

They were discussing when they would have to go home, and the older brother would have to leave Sunday at six p.m. so he could get to work on Monday at six a.m. Dad told him he'd be driving all night and he said it was OK, he was still young. Mom put baby sister to bed and baby brother was already asleep on the sofa and she carried him to bed and came back in with us. We were enjoying our conversation with Mary. She was so nice; it was like she was family already. All of us were getting tired. The weather was getting cooler, and it was getting dark earlier. I had to roll the folding bed out so Mary and I could sleep on it. Mom and dad went to bed. My middle brother and older brother went to sleep in middle brother's bedroom. Mary and I slept outside of my middle brother's bedroom.

Sunday morning, I heard mom get up about eight thirty and she was in the kitchen. It sounded like she was making dough for biscuits and cutting fresh slices of bacon off a slab they had at the store, and it was fresh. I got up when she was frying it because I loved to smell it frying. It was unusual dad wasn't up; he was tired from talking last night. It was after nine a.m., and I heard the brothers all getting up and washing their hands and getting dressed. Mom said she had never seen dad staying in bed that long. We heard him cough after she said that, and he was up and washing his hands. I heard Mary get up; she was tired also, but she had her makeup on, and her hair looked pretty, and she had another pretty dress on. I set the table and then went and got baby sister up. Mom said she gave her a bottle of milk at seven o'clock and she just woke up. I washed my baby sister's hands for her and sat her on the stool beside me, so I could help her eat. She was happy. We all loved the fresh bacon and the biscuits. We all ate fast because we liked what we had, and Mary said she would help me clean up the kitchen and she did a good job. We then went to the living room with all of them. Dad turned a preacher on and let all of us listen to a Surman.

After we listened to the preacher for an hour, mom told our older brother what happened to her when she tried to take dad's wallet to him that I had found in the swing. Pippy said, "It wouldn't have happened if I had been home. I would have taken it for you." She told him she had to get her false teeth next week because she broke them on the steps when she fell and cut her knee and had a long scar on it. He felt bad for her, and he remembered all the things that happened to all of us. Mary was listening to all of that, and she said that was terrible.

They began talking about going back to Ohio and somewhat dreading the trip. Mom told them she would make them a big sandwich of bologna and cheese to take with them when they leave, and they could buy something to drink when they stopped for gas. They said that was nice of her to do that. Mom said she would make some homemade vegetable soup they could eat about four o'clock and they said she was really nice to do that. She went back into the kitchen to do that. She had a lot of fresh vegetables, and she flavored it with some beef, and it smelled so good. We always loved her fresh vegetable soup.

Mary was talking to baby brother and asked if he would come and see them and he said, "Yes, and you can show me your big city." She said, "I will." In the meantime, mom had the vegetable soup ready, and we all sat down to eat a bowl of the best soup you could ever eat, and she fried some cornbread to go with it and Mary said she had never eaten fried cornbread, but she really liked it. The older brother said he had never had any since he left home. We were all happy having our dinner together. The older brother started looking at his watch and said, "We have one hour before we have to leave, and all our eyes were rolling. We felt bad knowing he would leave us again, but he was now a grown man, and he had a job now and he had responsibility. We were so happy he came to see us, and we wanted him to do what was right. Mom bagged up the sandwiches for them and they thanked her and took their clothes and personal things to the car. Older brother said, "We have ten minutes left, so we have to have a bear hug from all of you." We all hugged them, and mom and dad told them to be careful and to be safe on the road. Both younger brothers had tears in their eyes, and I did too. They got in the car and Mary thanked us for everything; she was really nice. They said they would try to come back within a year. Mom made us go back to the house and baby sister was still waving through the window, but they were gone.

Our Monday morning routine started again. We were off to school and dad didn't get up and we asked why, and mom said they put him on the afternoon shift. She didn't want to tell us because our brother was coming, and she didn't want that to be our conversation while he was with us.

We went on to school and we told our teachers about our visit with our brother, and they saw us being happy. It seemed like the shortest day at school we ever had. We still had our brother on our mind.

It was a big change to come home and not see dad. He left the house at three thirty and would not get home until twelve, so we wouldn't see him much until weekends.

After our company left our neighbor friends started coming back and visiting. We were happy about that.

One of our other neighbors' older sons came to visit. He is married and he brought his cousin with him to visit. I had never seen him, and they kept coming by every few days and I heard mom with them in the kitchen. They were talking low, and I couldn't hear them. They came again another day and we had to stay in the living room playing checkers and talking to each other, but I went up by the kitchen door and I heard the older boy say, "What happened to you is not going to happen to my wife; she is afraid to walk down the road since that happened to you." Then he said, "We have been watching from the woods to see what time the guy who runs the place leaves at night; it's between twelve and one a.m., usually." When he said that, I sat back down in the living room and mom looked in on us and the older boys told the kids with us they would walk them home when they were ready; and they all left.

We were tired and had to bathe before going to bed. I was happy we had already eaten before they came over, or we would have to eat very quickly. We were tired and nothing seemed right with dad not home. I saw mom take his gun and put it on her side of the bed and she said, "Your dad will be home at twelve midnight. He won't wake you up, he has a key and I put his plate of food in the Frigidaire; so good night to you and say your prayers. I will talk to you in the morning."

I woke up at five forty-five and heard mom in the kitchen and she told me to wake my brother for school. He was tired from playing checkers with his friends. He washed his face to wake up; I had already washed my face and hands and mom had our plates on the table. We had bacon, eggs and toast and we were happy with that. I asked if we could open the bedroom door and see dad and she said OK but don't open the door wide. We opened it and saw he was in bed and got our coats and left for school. Mom gave us a hug and said be careful.

We were happy to get to school and see everybody. We didn't like the idea that we couldn't see dad when we came home from school. It was strange and lonely, but the neighbor boys came to see us and asked mom if we could go to their house and she said we could, and she sent a note to their mom to send us home in an hour, and she did. They had an older sister and their mom and sister talked to me, and the boys were in the living room playing with race cars. We had a good time with them. We had some schoolwork to do at home and mom made us hamburgers and fried potatoes. After we ate, she told us to do the homework we had from school, and we done that. She said we could wash ourselves up with our wash pans tonight and we did. Mom gave my baby sister and younger brother a bath, and they were tired. I read them a story from the story book, and they fell asleep, and mom carried them to bed.

Mom let me and older brother stay up a little while longer and she talked to us about school and how important it was for us to get good grades. Then she turned the radio on to hear the news and we went to bed.

The next morning, I woke up at the same time and woke my brother up and mom was in the kitchen. She made us some cocoa, gravy and biscuits, and we really liked that. We were approaching fall and the leaves on the trees were colorful and the sun was going down behind the mountains, and it was getting dark faster and darker when we rode the bus to school. It seemed time was going faster in the fall and winter. The bus driver whizzed us to school, and we wasted no time getting off the bus. We were happy with our teachers; they worked teaching more than one class, HARD.

They really had the classrooms under control and sometimes they paddled some kids and the parents approved of it. We had a big stove in the classroom and one boy volunteered to put the wood in the stove and keep it burning to the end of the day. It kept us warm in the winter. We are missing seeing our dad and we like him home with us, but he must do what the supervisor says.

The boys at school said they would come see us again today after school and that made us happy. We quickly ran home when we got off the bus and told mom to let us eat fast, and she did. We told her the neighbor boys are coming over again. She smiled and said OK. The older neighbor boy came in his car and his cousin was with him and they picked the two younger boys up and brought them to the house and mom told us to stay in the living room and we had coloring books, and we all were coloring.

"I WAS VERY SCARED!"

I was through coloring, and I let my little sister color some on the bottom of the page. It made her happy. I got the race cars out for the boys; that's what they liked most, so they could make a lot of noise.

Mom told me to come to the kitchen and I did. The neighbor boy and his cousin told me I had to wrap something for them, and I said OK. They opened a bag and pulled something out of the bag, and he had gloves on. They told me to get some more bags out and to wrap the stuff he got out in three bags, separately. I said, "No", and my mom got my dad's belt and made me do it. I said, "It looks like dynamite", and they said no. They told me to go back into the living room and I did, but I came back up behind the door and I heard the older boy saying if it doesn't go off, they won't check a kid's fingerprints, so we don't have to worry. He told mom to call me back in there and make me swear to God I won't say anything.

"SWORN TO SILENCE!!!"

She called me back and the older boy said for me to hold my right hand up and swear to God that I wouldn't tell anyone; and I had to do it, or mom would use the belt on me. I was scared but didn't know what they would do. They said they would go in the woods across from the juke joint and check what time the man would leave for the last time tonight. They had been blowing horns at night and screaming and making a lot of noise and people were complaining. Mom was still sitting at the table, and they were too, and I was back up by the door and the older boy said we will put the dynamite behind the jukebox and that will scare them out of there. I was very scared but couldn't do anything about it. The older boys told the younger ones to get ready to go and they drove them home. My mom said don't talk to anyone about this and I said I won't. I couldn't even tell my dad.

I had a lot of anxiety over this, I was scared for a long time, and I didn't know when they would do that. I can't remember what night it was; it seemed like it was on a Monday or a weekend night, but I'm not sure. I heard the explosion, and I was frightened so bad I was hugging my pillow and crying and afraid to sniffle my nose and wake any of my family up. None of them woke up but me. I was nervous and not sleeping well at all, expecting this to happen. I think it was in the early morning hours and I don't remember going to school afterwards. I remember mom up first, as usual, and I got up and I told her I heard an explosion and she said, "Are you sure?" I said, "Yes." She started whispering to me and said don't say anything to your dad about this and I said OK. It was about fifteen minutes later, and dad was up washing his face and hands. He said good morning, and I asked him if he slept well, and he said yes. I heard the older brother get up and he carried little sister in, and younger brother followed.

Mom put breakfast on the table, and everyone got ready, both brothers were trying to get all the sausages they could eat; I never liked it, so I just had eggs and potatoes with a biscuit. That was enough for me. After we all ate, dad and the boys and baby sister all went into the living room, and he was talking to them, and mom and I cleaned the kitchen up; and went to the living room with them and dad turned the radio on, and mom looked over at me and I looked down at the floor. The music went off and the news came on. They were talking about the explosion, and I was very nervous. The man who leased the place was talking about the jukebox getting blown up and he said he jumped out of bed; so, I realized he had been staying there all along, it had to be another man that helped run the bar who the guy's thought was him. That was scary. It was the other man that left at night. THANK GOD nobody was hurt! Dad said, "I wonder who done that?" He had heard the neighbors talking about all the noise that was made down there and he thought they were mad.

I just wanted to forget all of this. I lived my life in fear and mom and dad were always fighting over him drinking, but it seemed like after the juke joint was blown up, he wasn't drinking very much. I think we were all scared for a long time. It was hard to get over the house on fire and them getting water to throw on the flames, but they got it put out, but we couldn't erase it from our memory. We were all still lonely after the older brother had left us. The weather was getting cooler and the trees in the mountains were nearly bare; that's when the pine trees showed up really green and pretty.

My younger brothers got their little race cars out and they made a lot of noise with them, and little sister was playing with her doll and talking to it; she was always good. Dad was tired of the radio, and he got the paper off the porch and was reading it and mom asked me to help her make some cookies and we went back into the kitchen. It took about an hour to make the cookies and they had peanut butter and chocolate in them, and they were really good. Mom had her false teeth, and she was happy she could chew the cookies. I asked mom if we could go to town and she said to ask my dad and I did, and he said if that's what you want to do. We all hurried to get ready, and we got in the car and headed to town. We had to pass the juke joint and dad slowed down beside it and you could see a big hole where the jukebox blew up and it made me nervous seeing that. We finally got into town, and we had to put our coats on; it was windy and cool. We walked a few blocks looking into store windows and I asked if we could get a chili dog and a milkshake and dad said yes, so we went in and sat in the booth and ate our chili dogs and milkshakes. Mom asked me if I planned this, and I said yes; I was tired of washing dishes. We all were tired of all the stress.

"BROTHER TO MARRY NEXT WEEK"

Our brother and Mary will be married next week but we won't be there because dad gets his two-week vacation in July every year and when we are out of school.

Mom said our oldest brother and his wife will come down in about two weeks. Our other brother told her when he left so we can be happy again.

We have been doing good in school and my younger brother says he will start school next year and he can ride the school bus with us. He is very anxious to start school. We haven't heard from our aunt in a while. Her husband must be working because she hasn't written to us lately. Mom will have to write to her and see if she is OK. The sun is going down very quickly so we must take our baths and get ready for bed. We have two tubs, and we get done faster if we use them both, so we did that. We were tired after our baths and we got our pajamas on and sat in the living room with dad, and we worked on our puzzles until we got tired, and it doesn't take long. We were batting our eyes and mom carried younger brother to bed and older brother wanted to go also; he was really tired, so he went by himself, and mom went to cover him up and came back. The news went off and we went to bed.

We all got up at nine a.m. this Sunday morning. When the weather gets cool in the mountains, we seem to get sleepy earlier. I told mom I would take care of the kitchen and she got a break. I told my older brother to ask if we could go see the neighbor boys and their older sister and she said she would write a note to their mom to send us back in one hour, so we agreed. I never had any girls my age that lived near me. Our younger brother went with us, and our friend's mom said he was a good-looking boy and very nice and he was smiling. We played checkers with them, and younger brother was coloring in their coloring book; he liked that. I was talking to their older sister, and she said she had one year to graduate; that time went fast. I asked their mom how many minutes we had left, and she said fifteen and I looked up on the wall and they had a big clock, so I was watching it because mom wouldn't allow us to be late. I told my brothers it was time to go, so they helped them put everything away and we said bye to them. We hurried back home, and mom told us to bring some wood in for the fireplace. It was October, but chilly. We will have a busy week at school having tests this week and they will be taking school pictures, so we will have to get our best clothes out to wear.

While we were gone, mom was making her vegetable soup with chunks of beef in it. It took a while because she let it simmer slowly and it was always good. We bathed ourselves early and put our pajamas on and sat in front of the fireplace. We liked looking at the fireplace and it warmed us up. Mom told us to get our school clothes ready for tomorrow and we did. Finally, the soup was ready and we had cornbread with it, and we thanked mom for it and she said to go to the living room with our dad, he will be listening to the news; and if we would get the big story book out she'd read us all a story by the fireplace when she got out of the kitchen. She read us a story and we were sleepy and went to bed.

"OH, HAPPY DAY!"

We were anxious to know what day our pictures were to be taken and we said our prayers and the Pledge of Allegiance, and then asked our teacher what day they will take our pictures and she said Friday. We were happy because we would send our brothers one and some other relatives. Many times, during mining strikes we could not have our pictures taken because we didn't have the money to pay for them. We were happy to hear they will take our pictures Friday. We couldn't wait to get on the school bus and tell our mom that. Our dad will be on the afternoon shift until December first. We hope the time goes fast; we don't see him much.

Mom got a letter from our aunt, and she said her husband is working and the other little boy she had is now eight months old and that she will try to come see us Christmas. That put a smile on our faces. I don't know why all the trauma we went through made us so close with our aunt and older brother, but we think about them a lot. It's like we lost them after they left, and we want to find them again.

This week seems to be going slow because we want our pictures taken. Our post office is just below the school and mom asked me to check the mail for her after I had my lunch and I got it for her; a letter for her and dad from our older brother and I wasn't allowed to open it, so I put it in my coat pocket until we got to catch the bus. We were anxious for them to read it to us. We got off the school bus and ran to the house and I handed it to her. She immediately opened it and read it to us. He said he changed the time, he is now coming this weekend, so it's the day after picture day. That made us happy, and his wife will be with him. Mom left the letter for dad to read when he got home at twelve midnight, when he warmed his food up. The letter was on the table.

Mom said her and dad would do the grocery shopping Thursday before he goes to work. She started cleaning the house on Wednesday, washing and ironing on Thursday, so everything would be clean.

Today is Wednesday, so we only have two more days for our pictures and Saturday our brother will come, and we won't be so lonely. Mom made us some French Toast and hot cocoa and we quickly were off to school. The bus driver always whizzed us to school, and we all liked that. We all got off the bus fast and ran to our classrooms and we said our prayer and the teacher began assigning us our work for the day. Then she assigned the other class their work for the day (she taught two different classes all the time). It wasn't long until our lunch bell rang, and we were all outside. It was cool, but sunny and we were all talking about our pictures. We wanted it over with. It wasn't long until the teacher rang the bell, and we went back in and finished our work. She assigned us to put our arms on the desk and our head down on our arms and rest while she graded our papers, and we did it.

She graded both classes papers and passed them out for us to take home. She told us to get our books and our papers and then she rang the bell, and we seen our bus was waiting for us and we hurried up and got on. We were happy because we both got an A+, and we wanted to show mom. We were soon getting off the bus again and anxious to show mom the grades we made. She said that our dad would be happy to see them. She said our baby sister and brother already had their baths and we could take ours before we eat dinner, and we did that in a hurry. She told us to put our pajamas on and we did, and we all followed her to the living room, and she turned the radio on to listen to the news. My baby sister and brother went to sleep right away and older brother and I went to bed and mom turned the radio off and went to bed.

The next morning, Thursday, Mom got us up about a half hour early. She made us gravy, biscuits and fried bologna and we loved it. She said she was going to wash the windows inside only because they would frost up outside and she had a lot of ironing and cleaning to do. She always kept a clean house. She told us to hurry up before we missed the bus; we were sleepy; she woke us up early. We grabbed our coats and lunch, and we were out the door. Our bus driver whizzed us to school. We really liked him.

We all got off the bus fast and went to our classrooms and the teacher seemed happy that we hurried up; she was sometimes tired. She told us to write a short story and that would be part of our English grade and we liked that.

We finally got some sunshine through the school windows and that made us more alert, and we finished our stories and turned them in. The teacher rang the bell for lunchtime, and we grabbed our lunch and went outside. We appreciated the sunshine; it warmed us up and made us happy. It wasn't long and the teacher was ringing the bell again for us to come in. We all wanted this day over. We were tired. My brother asked if he could ring the bell for when we go home and the teacher said yes, nobody had been asking lately. We all got seated and she said we could draw a picture of our house and she was grading the other classes' stories they had written. We were all anxious to go home and get our best clothes out for tomorrow.

"FRIDAY!"

My mom had pin curled my hair last night like all the moms do, and we wore our best clothes for our pictures to be taken and my brother wore a little bowtie and a white shirt. We looked in the mirror and I had a lot of curls and my mom put something on my brother's hair to keep it stiff. We happily left with our lunch in hand and our coats on. We were anxious to see the other kids on the bus, and they dressed up as much as they could.

The bus driver told us we all looked good. He was always nice to us, and we were all behaved on the bus, and he told us to smile big for our pictures as we got off the bus.

We quickly ran in the schoolhouse and our teacher said the camera man would be here at nine a.m. and set up everything. She told us we didn't have to do anything today, but we must keep our conversations quiet. She said our classroom will be in the morning and the other will be in the afternoon, and in between we will go to lunch. The camera man arrived at eight thirty and was setting up all the equipment and the lights. They take their time, that's why they take so long. I was with the first group and the second group will be this afternoon, then that will all be over and done. Our teacher is ringing the bell for lunch time and our first group is finished, and we were happy to get it over with. We were all anxious to go outside and have our lunch and walking around in the cool air felt good. We had a little rock wall where we sat to have our lunch, and we shared it with each other. We were all talking about Christmas. It was two months away and the teacher rang the bell again. They must finish the pictures.

Everyone lined up again, and it was going faster because he didn't have to set everything up; it was all ready. We asked the teacher if she was going to have her picture taken and she said no. We wanted a picture of her, but she didn't want that, so we shut up.

The teacher is still letting us talk quietly while he's still taking pictures. We keep hearing him telling different kids to smile and the teacher said he only has nine more and he will be through. About thirty minutes later the teacher was ringing the bell and we wanted to go home.

The bus was out there, and we ran to it. The bus driver was always happy, and he got us home fast. As soon as he let us off the bus, we ran to the house. Our dad was still at work until midnight and mom had us take our baths while she set the table. She already made the others take their baths.

We quickly took our baths and put our pajamas on and sat down at the table with baby sister and brother. All of us were tired and mom told us to go sit on the couch and we did. Mom came in and carried the two younger ones to bed. It was starting to get dark, and I went to bed; that left the older brother and mom up listening to the news. I don't know when they went to bed.

Saturday morning arrived, and Mom and I got up at the same time, six fifteen. I wanted to wake up early, knowing our oldest brother and his wife would be coming. We hadn't seen her yet; they had already got married and didn't tell anyone until recently. I got myself dressed up and helped mom make breakfast. She fried extra bacon and made extra biscuits and gravy for older brother and his wife and said she would only have to fry eggs so they could eat. We had everything set and I heard dad coughing when he got up and he woke up the rest of the family and they all washed their hands and came to the table. Dad was dressed, but the two brothers and baby sister had to get dressed after eating, so I helped her; but the boys dressed themselves and did a good job. Mom and I cleaned up the kitchen and dad turned the news on, and he was dressed up pretty good. Mom had her hair fixed and she still had her housecoat on, but changed to a dress and she looked neat and good. We made the beds, and everything looked good. We were waiting for them to come. We asked if we could go back with them and mom said no, you must finish school in the mountains.

We were all sitting in the living room, and we heard a horn blowing and we looked out and it was a new car, and we knew that was them. We all went to the front porch to greet them, and they walked up the steps and we grabbed our brother hugging him and he introduced his wife to us, and we all went to the living room and sat down. Mom asked if they had eaten and they said no, so mom headed to the kitchen to warm the food up and make eggs to go with it.

We went with them to the kitchen while they ate and mom and dad had coffee again and he told us his wife's name was Nina, and she was beautiful with long blond hair and blue eyes and a great personality. Our brother had gained a little weight and he looked really good. His wife said she had never been to the mountains, and she thought they were beautiful.

Dad told them we would take her to our small town and let her see it. We have two theaters, and all the people are friendly. I washed up the dishes after they got up. All of them went to the living room to talk, and I soon joined them. Dad asked them if they wanted to see the town and Nina said yes and older brother said he wanted to take his new car and let us ride with them and that's what we wanted. We loved new cars. My baby sister rode with mom and dad. We stopped at the drugstore, and we got out and went in and sat down in a booth and dad bought all of us a milkshake. We called that fun.

We were happy to have some family with us. We sat in the booth for a while talking and they finally asked if we were ready to leave and we said yes, so we got our jackets on and went for a short walk on the street. We walked around the corner and seen "Gypsy"! We were so excited, and she was too; we asked her where she had been, and she said she had had pneumonia for three months and she had lost a lot of weight. We kept hugging her, we were so happy to see her. We all loved her. She read everyone's hands and made everyone happy. Nina liked her, also. The older brother gave her some money. They remembered each other from long ago; she told him he was good-looking. We finally said goodbye to her, and she said she would see us again. We all headed to the cars; they were parked together, so we all got in and headed home.

Nina asked if she could go up in the mountains behind our house and big brother told her not to because it was late fall and the burs would stick to her clothes and get in her hair, and she didn't want that. We all got out of the cars when we got home, and we sat in the living room talking a lot. Dad got a deck of cards out and Nina, big brother, mom and dad played poker, and they were laughing a lot. The younger brothers played with their race cars and my baby sister went to sleep. Mom quit playing cards and put a beef roast in the oven with potatoes and carrots and came back and sat down. We were all a little tired and dad and older brother went out and shot their guns toward the mountains; they enjoyed that.

They stayed outside for about an hour, and when they came back in, they could smell that roast cooking. It smelled really good; mom seasoned it perfectly. Our baby sister woke up and everyone was talking and happy. Mom said dinner would be ready in about thirty-five minutes, so we sat in the living room talking and oldest brother said Mary and our brother who just visited us are going to have a baby and we said we didn't know that. He said not to say anything about it, and we all said OK.

Finally, we made it to the table, and everything was really good. The older brother said they would leave on Sunday evening because he had to work on Monday. He said he discussed it with our other brother, and he said night-driving had less traffic. We all sat at the table for a long time and mom cleared the table and got the dessert plates out and got two pies she baked out. Everyone was anxious to have the pies. They were lemon and we all liked them. We finally left the table and mom said she would clean the table up and told me to wash little sister up and put her pajamas on and let the boys use the wash pans and clean up. We all were hurrying up so we could sit in the living room and talk together. Nina went into the bedroom and put her long house coat on. We enjoyed talking with her; she was really nice. We asked mom if we could stay up late, and she said that depends on everybody else. Dad didn't turn the news on, and we liked that. We got to talk a lot with them.

My older brother was working in a car plant, and he was telling dad how they make cars and dad had a lot of questions. They were enjoying their conversation and Nina was talking to mom and us kids. She told us a lot about her family and said they were living in the city but looking for a farm with land. She said she thought the mountains were beautiful, but she said our city was too small; something I always thought.

It was really dark outside in the mountains. It made you sleepy when you looked out. I was beginning to bat my eyes, but they were all talking, and I really liked Nina, so I stayed up for about another thirty minutes, and I told everyone good night and went to bed.

Sunday morning, we all got up about nine a.m. and everyone seemed happy. Dad said he would take us to the little Diner for breakfast and we quickly got ready and left. They cooked really good there. We all ordered eggs and bacon and dad ordered three big stacks of pancakes for us to put on our plates. Everyone loved the pancakes, and we had plenty to eat. Nina said if we ate much there, we would get fat. Everyone cleaned their plates good, and we were ready to go. We still were in two cars. Our younger brothers rode with older brother and Nina and me and my baby sister rode with mom and dad.

We finally got back home, and they started talking about going back to their home. Mom told them she would make them some sandwiches with the big beef roast to take with them on the road. They said they would like that and thanked her.

Mom got the picture album out and showed Nina pictures of our older brother and she said he always looked good. She seen pictures of him with a Korean girl when he was over there, and she didn't like that.

We were all talking, and they wanted us to come up and see them when school was out, and dad said it would be in July when he would get his vacation for two weeks. Nina said she would take us to the museums and to the park where they had all the rides from spring to late fall and we could have fun like we did before. There's not much fun in small towns; you must visit with your neighbors and the kids all play together and everyone knows each other, and people have respect for each other.

Everyone was still talking, and mom said she would heat the roast up and make sandwiches for all of us and a big salad and she had so much meat left they could have sandwiches to take with them.

It was after four thirty and they were leaving at six p.m., just like the other brother, so mom had me helping her in the kitchen and we quickly had everything ready. Everyone washed their hands, and we sat down to eat. We had a huge bowl of salad, and I chopped it full of everything. Everyone was filling their salad bowls up and they seemed like they liked it. We had one big pie left and mom cut it for us, and we all had a piece. They said it was the best pie they ever ate.

Big brother was looking at his watch and he said it was five thirty p.m. We must be on the road at six p.m. Mom told me to get the sandwiches out and put them in a bag for them and they already had their clothes together. I was hoping the younger brothers wouldn't throw a fit as usual. The older brother told them to take the lunch bag to the car for him and two shirts and they took them for him. He was keeping them busy.

Finally, he told them they had to go, and I saw tears in their eyes.

We all hugged them and kissed them on the cheek and said bye and the younger brothers ran into the house crying. We all followed them in, and they were sitting on the couch crying a little. It wasn't as bad as the last time. Dad turned his news on, and he was happy to do it.

Little sister wanted her pajamas on, and I got them for her; she was sleepy, and we knew she would go to sleep on the couch. Mom told me and brother to take a bath and get ready for school in the morning, so we hurried to do that, and we were tired too. We all soon gave up and went to bed.

We are off to school again and dad's still on the afternoon shift, so we won't see him when he comes home. Mom told me to check the post office to see if we got mail and I checked and we got two letters: one from our aunt, and one from our other brother. I gave the letters to mom, and she read our aunt's first and she was asking if we could get middle brother to come at Christmas and we could all be together for a few days. Mom said she didn't know if she could do that, but she would try. My middle brother said he hopes he can come.

We started talking about all of us being together again and that sounded good to us, but we will have to wait and see. I wish dad was back on the day shift and I think he wants to be. We don't have a car at home, or him to drive us, so we must stay home in the evenings, and we are bored and scared.

We had our dinner, homemade vegetable beef soup, a salad and milk and cornbread. We loved it. Mom had baby sister bathed and younger brother is now bathing himself and that helps mom some. I take care of myself, and my school brother takes care of himself, so things are getting easier for mom. I told mom I want dad to teach me how to drive and she said maybe he will. It gets dark so fast after we come home from school. We get our homework done and it's time to go to bed. The days seem so short because it gets dark so fast in the mountains. We all want dad back on the day shift, but he can't force it, so we just have to forget about that. We all went to bed except mom, she stayed up to listen to the news and we didn't know when she went to bed. I know she puts dad's food in the fridge.

We were tired and mom had to make us get up and it was cold outside, and we would like to stay home, but that's something we never ask her because she said she wanted to get us educated because she had a hard life herself. She made us some hot cocoa, eggs and fried potatoes and I made toast for us.

We hurried out the door wanting to get the day over with. We were bored. Our bus driver whizzed us to school as usual and it was a dreary day. All day it looked like it would snow. Our teacher said we didn't have to eat our lunch outside if we didn't want to, so we stayed in.

Lunchtime was over and we had to get back to the books. Our teacher said we would have our testing next week, and we had to be ready for it. It wasn't long until she rang the bell, and we were anxious to get out the door.

"SURPRISE!!"

We were running to the bus and the bus driver was happy as ever to whizz us home. We got off the bus and headed home and when we topped the hill, we seen dad's car at home and didn't know why. We started running and mom seen us through the window and opened the door. We wanted to know why dad was home and he explained that an older man who had been injured in the mines retired and they let dad take his place and he was happy, and we were too.

We started feeling better knowing that dad would be home at night with us and have his car home too. We quickly ate our dinner and took our baths. We done our school homework, and we were happy to go into the living room with dad and stay on the sofa while he listened to the news. Both, little sister and brother went to sleep as usual, and we soon went to bed. I don't know when mom and dad went to bed.

My brother told the teacher at recess time that dad was back on the day shift. I saw him talking to the teacher and he told me what the teacher said. She told him she was happy for him.

The teacher had a big box in the room, and we asked what was in it, and she said that our pictures were in it, and she would pass them out after lunch; our names are on the packets they are in. Our teacher was ringing the bell for lunch, and she said we could stay in or go out, it was cold outside and most of us stayed in. It wasn't long and all of us were back in our seats waiting to get our pictures. The teacher had me come up to her desk and she counted out ten packets of pictures and told me to pass them to the right people. She also had a boy and another girl helping, and soon, they had all been passed out. We were all looking at our pictures and showing them to each other. Our mom's usually chose who would get pictures in our family. Our teacher gave us another thirty minutes to converse about our pictures and we were happy. She was grading papers from the other class, and we finally were being quiet and tired. She finished grading the papers and not many things were left to do. She got up from her desk and went to ring the bell. We all ran to the school bus and the driver asked us to hurry because the door was open. We were soon on our way home. We got off the bus and ran home with our pictures. Mom said they looked like they took well, and dad said they looked good to him. Mom would decide who would get a picture of us and we were allowed to give one picture away to our best friend.

Tomorrow it's supposed to snow, and everyone is talking about Christmas and praying that a strike will not come; it has happened many times and hurt all of us.

We woke up to snow and dad went out and measured it with his yard stick and said it is four inches deep; we would like that if we could go out and play in it. It's now November and they will be putting the Christmas lights up on the stores and have Christmas trees inside them. We asked mom to make us a quick breakfast and she said asked what we wanted. We told her French Toast, cereal and cocoa, and she said OK.

We went to the living room with dad, and we asked if he would take us to town so we could see them put up the lights and he said yes, oh happy day!

Mom told us to come and eat and we were eating fast and got ready faster, "We loved "yes" answers." We were soon in town and some of the lights were already up, but they were still stringing them. Baby sister was smiling when we got out of the car. We all liked the snow if it wasn't too deep.

Dad seen some of his miner friends and they all started talking to him and we walked on. We went to one store, and they had a big Christmas tree lit up. My little sister wanted to touch the bulbs and mom told her they were "hot", and she said OK.

Dad finally caught up with us and we went out on the sidewalk and little sister pointed to the drugstore and said, "Ice cream." Dad said it was too cold, and she said, "No." So, we headed to the drugstore. We sat in the booths, and we ordered ice cream cones, and we were happy! We sat there for about an hour, and we ordered some more water and two napkins to wipe my little sister's mouth and younger brother's, also. They ate chocolate ice cream and had it all over their mouths. We cleaned them up and they were ready to go; and they asked when we could go again. Dad said maybe soon. The sun came out on the way home and the snow was sparkling and beautiful and the pine trees in the mountains looked good with snow on them and they smelled good with snow on them.

In the summer when you walked into them, the brown nettles were on the ground, and you could still smell the trees and they gave you shade and a close to God feeling. This is not say-so; try it yourself and you will understand and appreciate them.

We made it home and the snow didn't melt, and the sun went into the clouds, but everything still looked pretty.

Dad stayed outside for a while putting firewood on the end of the porch so we could reach it. Dad put some logs in the fireplace, and it got really warm in the living room. Mom was in the kitchen making her own vegetable beef soup and cornbread. We loved it. She said it had to be cooked fifteen more minutes and we could come to the table and eat, after we washed our hands. We all heard that and started washing our hands right away. We were ready to eat that soup. She called us about ten minutes later.

We were happy mom made the soup. We all hurried to eat dinner so we could sit in front of the fireplace and dad was listening to his news. We enjoyed the fireplace. Mom finished up the kitchen and the boys washed up in the wash pans and I bathed baby sister and I put her pajamas on her, and she went to the sofa. The boys finished washing up and put their pajamas on, and I washed the wash pans, and I used one for myself, so we all had a quick bath. We were all tired and wanting to go to bed. "We" could go, but mom said she had to wait until all the wood burned up in the fireplace so no sparks could jump out and catch something on fire. So, all of us went to bed but mom.

We all rested well last night, and we all were up at nine a.m. and the snow was still on the ground. Mom was talking about moving to town and dad agreed. Mom wanted to get away from that house, she had bad memories and felt like if she moved, she would feel better, so they started looking in the ads in the newspaper and found one but would have to call the owners on Monday. We didn't have a phone at the time. Everyone called from the drugstores or gas stations, and he went to the drugstore and made the call. He was pleasantly surprised it was one of the miners; he would have to pay a month in advance, and he said OK. He told mom and she was happy, and we were also. We had to change schools. All we had to do was take our report cards with us and birth certificates to the teachers and we did that, and we were enrolled. It was just a little over a mile to school, so we still rode the school bus. Dad checked with mom's cousin who run North American Van Lines and he gave dad a good deal. Dad needed help to move.

Dad sent our brothers a telegram and asked them to come help him move, and they sent one back and said, "We will be there!" Dad set the move for next Saturday and they arrived on Friday evening. They took time off from work and didn't have their wives with them; and they were organizing things that had to be taken out first. They rode together in my older brother's car. We were all up early on Saturday morning. Mom had made bologna and cheese sandwiches and told them dad would take us to the family drive-in and we could go inside and eat dinner after the move.

Mom had me give my little sister and the two younger brothers their sandwiches and we had cartons of milk. I kept them out of the way, and we sat on the floor and ate. Mom and dad went into the kitchen and two chairs were in there, so they sat down to eat, and our brothers stood and ate. They were so fast they had everything in the truck and dad drove it. My oldest brother drove us in dad's car, and my other brother drove oldest brother's car.

It was the quickest move I ever saw. We were all happy and dad had the boys move the table and chairs to the new kitchen and told us kids to go and sit in the kitchen and stay there, and we did.

I peeked around the corner, and they had the living room set up and were moving beds in; they were fast. Mom said she was timing them, and they were through in two hours and fifteen minutes.

Dad said he could never have done that by himself. They had mom directing where to put things and she was putting things away. They really did a neat job. Little sister was going around saying, "This is not my house", and we were laughing at her.

Dad said he would drive the truck back and older brother followed him in his car and brought him back. Mom put sheets on the beds while they were gone, and the beds are ready for us. When dad got back, mom told him we needed to all wash our hands and go to the drive-in restaurant and go in and sit down to eat, and he said to give him about a half hour to rest a little and she said OK. He fell asleep on the sofa, and they let him sleep another fifteen minutes and told him to get up and let's go eat. He was still tired, but he got up. We all got in the two cars and drove to the drive-in and got seated. They had homemade food and pies and cakes.

We all sat down, and the waitress took our orders, and we were happy the move was over. Dad said we must change our address at the post office and his driver's license.

Our waitress was coming over and she had a lot of food on the big tray and had to go back for more. It all looked so good. It was homemade.

"BROTHERS WENT HOME AND ARE COMING BACK SATURDAY"

We are anxiously waiting for Christmas to come. We will have a lot of relatives; both brothers and their wives, and a newborn baby girl, and they will all be bringing Christmas gifts, and we must go shopping for them.

We couldn't go to Mary and older brother's wedding but now they are bringing the newborn baby, and our oldest brother is coming with his wife. They will stay one day and Christmas day with us, and then go to her family's reunion after they exchange gifts with us. Our aunt and her little boys will be coming, too. We will be happy, and we are going shopping for gifts for all of them tomorrow, and we will have them boxed and wrapped. We are going to bed early tonight and tomorrow will be busy for us. We are off for Christmas vacation, still. Our aunt will come in with the two little boys tomorrow and all the others will come after her. We are ready for all of them to come.

We were happy shopping, and we were all talking about what happened to us, and we just couldn't forget it. Mom always changed the subject when she could. We have our Christmas gift shopping done. We bought our brothers nice watches, and we know they will like them. We bought our aunt's little boys' nice jackets. We bought our brother's wife's nice purses, all leather. We are all happy that we had money to do this. We are so happy we will all be together for Christmas.

Our aunt is supposed to arrive today, and we will be happy to see the little boys. Dad is supposed to pick her up at six p.m., and I wanted to go with him, but mom wanted to go, so I stayed home and watched my brothers, and we were happy and little sister was sleeping. It is five thirty and my brother is watching the clock and we all had dinner already and mom put food up for them.

I told the boys to be quiet and let little sister sleep and wait until they got back with our aunt, and she would be surprised, and they said OK. We heard a horn blowing and my brother looked out and said, "It's dad! They are here!" We were so happy, and they were as happy as we were to see us. The little boys were very cute, quiet and well mannered. My aunt had been waiting about a half hour; she said the bus was early. We were all so happy to see them. Mom helped them get their clothes and everything in the room they would stay in, and our aunt asked when our brother who helped her run the business would be here, and dad told her tomorrow. She said, "I can't wait to see him." We told her his wife and baby will be with him and she said, "Great!" Mom told her she had food for them, and she said they ate at the last bus station.

"BROTHERS ARE BACK!"

About an hour later, both of our brothers arrived, and everyone was so happy to be together. My aunt and older brother that had run the beer joint for dad, couldn't stop hugging each other and they were crying. They never forgot what happened. Mary was holding the newborn baby, and it was asleep. We all were happy to see the baby; she is so tiny and pretty. Mary asked if she could heat her bottle and mom said sure and heated it for her. She thanked mom. We all liked her a lot and she looked really good and dressed nicely. The other brother's wife's name was Nina, and we loved her also. They both are well mannered and kind, and we love them. We have a house full of family and the small boys of my aunt's are trying to sit by Mary and the baby and she knows they want to touch her, and she said you can kiss her on the top of her head, and they were happy and smiling. Mom told them they could sleep in the larger bedroom because the baby's bassinet must be beside Mary, and Mary thanked her.

We are so happy our aunt and our brother got to see each other. We will be giving out the gifts we bought for all of them tomorrow. We were all really tired and they were tired from driving. Mom asked Nina and older brother if they wanted something to eat and they said no, they had eaten dinner at a big restaurant on the road. We all were tired, and mom said if they wanted to go to bed, they could. We all agreed to go to bed.

"CHRISTMAS GIFT DAY!"

Waking up from smelling the bacon, I got up slowly so I wouldn't wake the younger ones up. Mom was cooking as usual, and the two older brothers were in the living room drinking coffee she had made them. I talked to them briefly and went into the kitchen to help mom. I quickly set the table and mom was taking biscuits out of the oven; that's what they all loved, homemade biscuits. I heard my brothers' wives talking. They were completely dressed and looked very nice. Dad was peeking around the corner, and he was already dressed, and went straight to the kitchen for a cup of coffee and then sat down with the older boys. My sister-in-laws went in the kitchen and Mary was making the baby a bottle and she quietly took it in to her and sat in a chair holding her while she nursed her bottle. The baby went back to sleep and Mary went back into the kitchen. I heard someone else getting up and it was our aunt. She was quiet and she got dressed and went to the kitchen. They were taking up the food and putting it on the table and everyone, but the kids were up, and mom said to let them sleep, and that we could eat and then wake them up. We all agreed because they will want to open their gifts. We all began eating and my brother next to me came dressed and washed his hands and we told him to be quiet and he said OK and began eating. My aunt's little boys were the last ones to get up and we had almost finished, and the younger boy was looking for mommy. His mom met him in the hallway and the older boy was washing his hands. They were good little boys. Everyone had a few minutes at the table together. The boys were trying to eat fast so they could get the gifts. Our baby sister, we nearly forgot about her, she is so quiet. Mom went in to get her and she was happy as usual and said, "I am hungry." Mom took her to the table, and they were all talking about gifts.

They were not eating very much because they wanted to open gifts. They quit eating and headed to the Christmas tree with the gifts under it in the living room. Dad said to let the kids open theirs first, and they were all happy. The best two kids were my baby sister and my aunt's younger boy. They opened their gifts real fast, and they were all "happy".

Dad suggested we let our older brothers and our aunt open their presents and mom passed all the gifts to the adults. Our brothers and their wives loved the gifts we got them. So, everyone was happy.

Our older brother wanted to pass mom and dad's gifts to them, and dad said OK, and they were happy with "everything" they got.

"HAPPIEST CHRISTMAS WE EVER HAD"

This was the happiest Christmas we ever had! Our sister- in-laws were the best we could ever have had; they are nice and have a sense of humor and they treat everyone good. All the children are behaved, and they all like each other. When they leave, we will be lonely.

The older brother and his wife will be leaving this afternoon, and they just decided that because they have a three-hour drive to her family's home. They need to leave and get there before dark because they have a family reunion every Christmas.

We don't want them to leave us, but they have this every year. This was the first time they visited us on Christmas. Mom told them she would make them a light lunch before they left, and they said OK. Mom got everything out of the freezer before we got up. She had a whole turkey and a big ham, mashed potatoes, green beans and we will make the big salad when she tells me to and cover it up. When she is ready, she will tell us. Dad and the older boys went outside and was shooting his guns for a while and the sun came out and it was getting a little warmer; we were happy for that. Finally, they came back in, and the kids were making a lot of noise with their toys. Mom, aunt and the two daughters-in-law were sitting at the kitchen table talking. Mom got up and hurriedly made older brother and his wife some hot turkey, mashed potatoes and green beans and she had hot rolls for them and told me to get two bowls for the salad and we got everything together for them to have a lunch before they left.

They quickly washed their hands and mom cut the pecan pie and the lemon pie for them. Everything looked so good.

They ate everything on their plates. They said everything was perfect! They kept thanking mom and they cleaned the table for us and put the dishes in the sink. They said they would leave in a half hour. We didn't want them to go, but they were obliged. They went back into the living room and the kids were all still playing with all the toys. They were full of energy.

Brother and sister-in-law told us they had to leave but they will come back in the summer and the kids didn't start to cry because we still have the other brother, his wife, and baby with us. We all hugged them and told them bye and told them to be careful and we loved them, and they got in their car and left. The kids never left the toys!

They finally fell asleep on the blankets. Then mom, our aunt and daughter in law quickly put dinner together for all of us and we had to wake the kids up to eat. They were all tired but washed their hands and came to the table. The kids didn't eat much but they all wanted some pie, so our aunt cut them each a small piece and they all ate it.

Our aunt told the kids to put their pajamas on so they wouldn't have to do it later. She had to help her younger son with his; and my aunt and me cleaned up the kitchen and mom and dad went to the living room with the kids, and they were playing again. My aunt reminded mom that her husband would be picking her up tomorrow and her and the kids would go with him to see his family and they would leave from there to Baltimore and after she leaves, our brother, his wife and the baby will leave the next day. Then we will be lonely again.

I think all of us were tired and we all wanted to go to bed, as the kids were quieter, and the sun had gone down. My mom and aunt had the kids go to bed first and they were really quiet, so we knew they were tired. We said good night and they didn't answer. We were all tired and we were dreading saying bye to our aunt. She stayed with us a lot when her crazy husband went to prison for check writing and no money in the bank. Dad didn't want to listen to the news and all of us went to bed.

Our aunt was up at six a.m. the next morning. She had two suitcases and a large leather shopping bag at the front door, and she had the boys' clothes they would be wearing draped on top of the suitcases. She went and got her boys up and washed the smaller one's face and the older one took care of himself. They were ready to go. Our aunt still had to fix her hair and she did that quickly. I saw mom coming through the hall and she asked our aunt what they wanted to eat for breakfast and my aunt answered, "French Toast, and that's enough." Mom got all of it ready with the coffee, and milk for the kids. They were happy. My older brother, his wife and the baby got up. Mary made the baby a bottle of milk and carried her back to the bassinet and propped her bottle and she went back to sleep. Finally, dad got up and he was happy that we had a small amount of food.

We all quickly ate and started getting up from the table and we heard a knock on the door and mom answered the door. It was our aunt's husband and he asked if they were ready to go and mom said yes. He picked up the suitcases and the large shopping bag and my aunt said bye to all of us. We all had tears in our eyes. The little boys ran out to their dad and older brother told our aunt he was so happy to see her, and she said likewise.

We all still felt the pain of what happened to us when dad ran those places. Even our younger sister was crying; she loved our aunt, also. Dad was sad but he didn't want her husband to come in and he felt bad for our aunt and wished her the best.

Tomorrow our brother, his wife and the baby will leave, so we want to make the best of everything today. Dad said he would take us to dinner at the place we all like and we all loved that. Mom had already cleaned up the kitchen, so we all decided we didn't want any lunch, so the kids wanted to play with some of their Christmas stuff again. Mom told them they can't go outside; she didn't want them to get their clothes dirty so we could go have dinner at the place with good homemade stuff. We are all happy, and we love the little baby. She's so good, and Mary is so nice. The kids are so happy playing with their gifts. Mary asked mom if she could have a picture of our older brother to keep when he was younger and mom gave her one, and she put it in her suitcase and thanked mom. Mary liked the mountains, but she didn't like our small town, and I was with her on that. A few hours went by, and the kids were still trying on clothes and looking at all the things they got, and they were happy. Dad asked if we were about ready to go to the restaurant, and we all said yes!

Mary was heating the baby a bottle and wrapping it so it would stay warm. We took both cars so Mary could feed the baby while the older brother was driving.

We were on our way to the restaurant we all loved. The waitress began to remember us, and we were seated fast. Mary said she had never eaten at a restaurant where everything was good until she ate there.

We were all in a good mood and the baby drank all of her bottle and went back to sleep. Newborns sleep a lot, always. The waitress is coming with our food now and it looks good. Mary laid the baby in the booth beside her, and she was sound asleep. We are all eating now, and everyone was happy with the food. We never ate our food fast; we chewed it slowly because it was so good. The kids wanted ice cream and we all wanted homemade pies. We all loved the lemon and chocolate the best, and that's what all the adults had. It was the best pie in the world!

We were all soon ready to go and the older brother picked the baby up and put her in Mary's arms, and we were all leaving the restaurant. It seemed a little warmer this evening and we are hoping for no more snow.

We all got in the house quickly and dreaded tomorrow when they would be leaving. Mom told me not to talk about it and I didn't.

The baby woke up and Mary said she would bathe her now and she would be clean to go home. Mom told us to go into the living room with dad and older brother and we did. The boys and baby sister were getting their toys out and seemed to be happy. I sat in the living room with dad and older brother talking with them. Mom stayed with Mary and the baby, and they were pouring bath water down the sink. Mary dressed the baby in her nightgown and took her into the living room. She put her on the sofa with a pillow in front of her and the baby was being quiet. The kids were still playing. Mom told them they'd have to go to bed in an hour and they didn't complain; they were tired. Mary and older brother had to take a shower and they hurried up and did that. I watched the baby when they took their showers, and she was very quiet. We were all tired and mom was batting her eyes and Mary was making a warm bottle for the baby and wrapping it up to stay warm. Mom took a shower and told me to go to bed, and I did. Mary had the baby in the bassinet, and she went to bed. Mom, dad and older brother were still up, and I heard mom say, "I'm going to bed." Then, I fell asleep.

The next morning, Mom woke us up with the bacon smell; it works every time. Everyone was up, except my baby sister and younger brother. Mary was making the baby a bottle and mom asked us all to not wake baby sister or our other brother, so we were staying quiet. Mom had me set the table and she poured every one of them their coffee and Mary had finished feeding the baby and put her on the sofa and we all sat down. We had a big breakfast and the older brother said they will be leaving about eleven a.m. and he said if we are quiet the younger ones will stay asleep, and they won't be crying. He was right. Mary, brother and baby were all in the car at eleven a.m. We hugged them bye and told them we were happy they brought the baby with them.

We were already lonely. The house seemed so empty. It was about twenty minutes and younger brother got up and woke little sister up and she ran to the window, looked out, and said, "They are gone!" Her and younger brother ran to their toys. We already miss having the little baby. She was so good. We miss all of them.

I was helping mom to wash bed clothes and clean up the house. We must be back at school on Monday. Everything is going well, and we have good grades. Dad said we will go see our brothers when we go on vacation in July. We said that's what we want. We haven't heard from them since they left. The daughters-in-law are probably visiting with their families. I asked mom if I could call Mary and she said OK. I called her, but no answer. I called my eldest brother's wife and got no answer. Mom said they are probably with their families like you said. We got a call back the next day from both sisters-in-laws, and they had been with their families, so we didn't have to worry about them, and they both said to thank mom for all the good food she made for them.

"THE WORST THING THAT COULD HAPPEN TO A FAMILY!!"

We are still happy that they came to see us. The phone was ringing, and dad answered it. He was turning white and looking sad, and mom said, "What's wrong?" He said to let him sit down and he'd tell her. She said, "OK." We all went into the living room, and he said, "Your brother is in jail." We were all gasping, and he said, "Pippy." He is the one that did everything for us and stayed the longest with us and we all were crying. Mom asked, "What did he do?" Dad said, "He is accused of shooting and killing Mary." We all said, "He didn't do it!" We were crying all day and looking at each other. We didn't know what to do. Our teachers were asking what was wrong because we are crying so much, and we said we can't tell you because mom said to not talk about it. They said OK. My heart was broken the next day going to school again crying, the neighbor kids asked if they could help us and we said no, and they quit questioning. We are having a hard time going to school and thinking about this. I wanted to go home and stay. We were on the bus again going home and we were tired. When we got home, mom had made us bologna sandwiches with cheese. She was tired and worrying over this, but she was still saying he didn't do this, and all of us were saying it. Dad got a letter from eldest brother, and they were opening it and I was looking and dad pulled a piece of newspaper out of it and he was saying eldest brother sent this and I was looking at the back of it and I said, "I see a picture of Mary. It's on the newspaper." Dad quickly began reading it and he was so nervous, and mom was looking so sad and crying. We all were crying again and couldn't do anything. I looked at dad and asked if we could go to her funeral and he said, "No. They think your brother killed her; they might call the police on us." We were all crying again, and I asked, "How can we get over this?" Mom said, "You can't." We don't know what to do. We are too upset to eat. Mom told us to take a shower. We don't want to eat; we are so scared. I didn't know what to do and we all took a shower and mom coaxed us to eat. We didn't want to. We all were scared, and we were wondering what the police might do to him. We asked dad how long they will keep him, and he said if they find somebody else who committed the crime, they will let him go, but we don't know how long that will take. We all went to bed early. We are so tired with worry.

The next morning, all of us had swollen eyes from crying. Mom made us a breakfast she knew we would eat, French Toast and cocoa, and we finished it fast. Dad left before us, but we were all up a little early. I dread seeing my teacher. She knows something bad happened and I can't tell her. Mom said don't tell this to anyone and I said I wouldn't. We quickly ran to the bus stop, and it was a cold morning. Our brother is still in jail, and we can't talk to him. We don't know what to do. We made it to school, and I haven't been talking much to anybody. They know something is wrong and we can't talk about it. We just can't be ourselves. I know the teachers are feeling bad for us; we are so quiet.

We came home from school and asked mom if she heard anything, and she said no. I asked if we could call eldest brother, and she said to wait a few minutes and dad would call him when he comes in. We need to know what happened. Dad came in right after she said that and asked her if she heard anything, and she said no. He was looking perplexed and very tired. He said they should know something by now and he was going to call eldest son, and he did. They were on the phone for over an hour, and he asked mom for a pencil and paper, and he was writing things down to tell us. Mom was setting the table, and she made her homemade beef stew with big chunks of beef in it, and she said it has to cool and your dad can tell us what older brother said. He said, "The police have an A.P.B. (all points bulletin) out on the color and make of the car." He explained that the police and a detective questioned the people across the street. They saw the men who grabbed her up and was trying to put her in their car, and she screamed, and they shot her. The man said they (the killers) got in their car and left quickly. They said they got out of their car and walked across the street and the man said he put his overcoat over her, and they called the police. This is what the people told eldest brother.

Now we know how it happened and it's so hurtful to think about it. We were all crying again. I'm sure her family cried a lot. The days are passing by fast and it's a big worry with no one knowing what to do. Our brother told dad that Mary's sister has their baby. They said she would keep it.

We have no way to find out anyway, we live far away. Several days have gone by and they are still trying to find the killers. My eldest brother said he will call us if anything changes. He is worried about this for the sake of the baby.

We are trying to console each other. Dad said tomorrow will be the eighth day and they haven't found them. Dad says the longer it goes, the less likely they will find them. We are all worried. Our eldest brother said Mary's sister says she is going to turn the baby in to the Catholic Orphanage Home and there's nothing any of us can do. That hurts our feelings, but we can't change it.

It is the evening of the eighth day and eldest brother was calling dad. He called the officer he had been talking to and they told him a state trooper was talking to two men who had just crossed the state line into Florida and the car matches the one the neighbor described. He searched their car and handcuffed them to the car and called for "backup" and was questioning them separately, taking one at a time to his police car handcuffed. Apparently, one of them thought he was getting questioned about a bank they had robbed and admitted it to him, and the policeman said, "We already know you robbed the bank, but we also know you killed a young woman." The officer's "backup" pulled in and the officer kept interrogating him and he admitted it and they all left to the police station. This was all what a policeman told our eldest brother. He has found out everything he can and called dad and told him what he found out and we appreciate our other brother telling us; we are so worried because we all know Pippy didn't do this. He was always nice to everyone. The eldest brother has kept a close watch on this and has written notes on what the officer has been telling him. He was so anxious to call dad; he knows how upset we are. Dad said, "They won't release him right away. They have to make sure everything is right, and they have to take him before the judge to be released." Finally, it happened, and he went to Mary's sister, and she told him she turned the baby in to the Catholic Orphanage Home and he would have to go there.

He asked eldest brother to go with him and he did. The nuns treated them very good, but they said you won't be able to see her and that she was going to be taken to another state to be adopted, and he was crying and saying, "I will find her," and the nun told him that she will have to find him when she gets older. He was crying again and saying, "I have lost my wife and my daughter, and I can't do anything!" My eldest brother said, "Let's go to my house and think about it. Is that OK?" He said yes. He was very upset, and he said, "I will have to call everywhere and try to find her." He had joined the Army and quit his old job, as he didn't like it. He was going to study and make a career of it and take Mary and the baby with him as soon as he could, but the Army checked up on him, and asked him to come in and he was so nervous and shaking. They said they wanted a doctor to check him and then they said he would have to take medicine and they discharged him. He came to see us, and his hands were very shaky, and he was losing weight and was shaking Mary's class ring on his key chain and was feeling terrible. We felt so bad for him. Mom told him she would keep the baby if he could get her, and he said the orphanage said he can never find her, but when she's older she can look for him; it really hurt him.

He continued searching for her and he finally would stop for a while and start back. He will never stop. He stayed with us a week and now he is going back. We hate it that he has to drive by himself home; but he says he can do it. We are all worried about him. He will be leaving in the morning when we are ready for school. I dread it. We all will be crying, and the teacher will see our eyes. Mom made us some beef stew and we all ate that, and we were all tired. We took our showers, and we were ready for bed. Dad listened to the news and went to bed.

We got up early and we didn't sleep well. We are all looking at each other and dad got up from the table and said, "I have to go." We all hugged him, and the older brother had tears in his eyes. Dad said, "We will come see you when we can." My older brother said OK. The older brother was set to go, and he gave us a hug and a kiss on the cheek, and we were all crying. Mom told him, "We'll try to come see you soon." We all said we love you and he said I love all of you, too, and he went out the door.

Mom told us to wash our faces in cold water and the tears might not show on our cheeks. We only had twenty minutes, and we were out the door. The neighbor kids were happy to see us. We had to be quiet because we couldn't talk about Mary, or our brother going to jail, being accused of her murder and we still can't.

Time is flying and mom said, "You only have about three months until school is out, not even that, if you take the weekends out. The weather
is still cool, and we may get a light snow, but I hope not."

We are still quieter than usual. It's such a horrible thing to tell anyone, and we don't want to talk about it. We want it to go away, but it never
will. My aunt had divorced and remarried. Her husband will be coming
down from Michigan and taking me back so I can work and make some
money to buy me some clothes. The big city has prettier clothes than the
mountains have and more variety. I will be working at the same restaurant I worked at before and the people already know me. Time is flying
and my uncle will be here in two weeks. After I get there, I will only stay
for two and a half months, then I'll go home for two weeks and leave for
Lexington with my scholarship and finish my education.

We went on to school. My youngest brother is still in grade school
and will pass to seventh grade, and the other brother Glenn, is in tenth
grade. He is begging mom and dad to sign for him to join the Army, and
they are refusing and telling him he must finish school. Time is going
fast, and school will be out soon. My younger brother asked me if I am
going to leave them like our brothers have already and I said when I finish
my education, I will have to for that. My little sister asked if I would come
back home and I said, "Yes, but I won't stay long." I told her I will have
to go to Michigan for a job after school. She asked if she could go with
me and I said, "Mom won't let you go. I have nobody to keep you when
I work." So, she didn't say anything else. My uncle will be here in one
more day and he will take me back with him. School is out and I grad-
uated, and both brothers have good grades, so mom and dad are happy.
Waking up early Saturday morning and my uncle came in last night, but
they didn't wake me up and I already have my clothes packed and uncle
said that was smart, and I said I was anxious. He knows I am anxious.
Mom made breakfast for us, and I fried some pancakes with the bacon
and eggs. We all enjoyed our food and when everyone had finished, I told
mom to go in the living room and rest and dad and uncle went up to the
little grocery store and gas station and uncle was pumping gas for people
and he said he liked it there.

Southern men, and mountain men, love to shoot their guns; so, dad
and uncle were shooting their guns that evening and mom and I were in

the store talking. I will have to be up early in the morning because my uncle must be at work Monday flying out to the Virgin Islands and St. Thomas. He is a dry good salesman. So, we were up Sunday morning at six a.m. leaving. Mom said, "Let's not wake the kids up", and we didn't. I hugged mom and dad and told them I loved them; and we were on our way. It took twelve hours for us to get to my aunt and uncle's house. We were tired, but I got clothes out to go get my job back and they were happy to see me, and I was happy to see them. They said I would get a small raise and still earn my tips and that made me happy. Time is going so fast. I'm working every day I can so I will be able to buy clothes and dad won't have to buy them for me. I'm happy working with some people I worked with before. It seems as if they wanted to help me, and I always helped them also. I got a letter from my brother who lost his wife and little girl. He is still sad and wondering where his little girl is, and still calling different states to try and find her. My mom has been a little sick and she is praying he will find her before she dies, and we are hoping for that also. It has nearly destroyed him. He is very nervous and trying to work, but we don't know if he is able to keep a job, but he is working right now. I must call him when I get time. My aunt said she will remind me.

My aunt said if I can get a day off, they will take me to the zoo, and I said OK, I will ask the next day. I asked if I could have a day off and they said, "Yes". I was so happy. I asked my aunt if Monday would be OK and she asked my uncle, and he said yes. I was so excited. I had never been to a zoo, and I needed a break. Today was Saturday and I will work today and tomorrow, and they will take me Monday morning at 10 a.m.

I finished my work, and in the morning, we will be at the zoo and my aunt's two little boys will be with us. The one will be in a stroller; they had been to the zoo before. I was the excited one because I wanted to see the gorillas and giraffes; I felt so happy.

We went to bed early, and my aunt said she would be up at six a.m. in the morning and cook breakfast for us, and we were happy.

The bacon smell woke us up. We were all anxious to get ready. I quickly got ready and put my aunt's dishes in the dishwasher. I didn't know how to turn it on; she turned it on, and she laughed at me. We didn't have them in the mountains yet. We were happy getting in the car and on our way.

My uncle drove us through the big city of Detroit, and I was stretching my neck looking at the skyscrapers (tall buildings). That's what they called them. I saw a big sign ahead. It said, "Detroit Zoo", and I was so excited. My uncle turned in and drove into a parking lot and a man charged him a quarter to park and gave him a ticket telling him where he parked. We were happy and I could hardly wait to see the gorillas. I pushed the stroller with the younger boy in it until I started seeing the animals and I loved watching the gorillas; they were really funny and did a few flips. They were really big. My uncle said, "Let's go in the big tent. The elephants will be doing a show."

We all loved the elephants. They did a big show for us; then the giraffes came out. One was a baby with its mom, and they were marching around the big circle. Next, we seen the monkey's ("chimps") and we wanted to get away from them. They were throwing dung and some of it came out of the cages smelling bad. Uncle suggested we let the little boys ride the merry go round and some little cars and we walked over to them, and he got their tickets and he put the older boy on the horse and he had to stand and hold the younger boy on the horse, but he loved it more than the older boy. We were all tired and my aunt suggested we go to a restaurant and uncle agreed, so he took us to a steakhouse, and we all ate well because everything was really good. We were all happy and I thanked them for taking me to the zoo. We all liked it. I tried to pay them, but they wouldn't let me. We were all tired and were ready for bed, and I have to work tomorrow, so I have to get to sleep. So, we all went to bed.

One morning, my uncle got the calendar down and he was checking to see when I had written in it that I had to go home and he said we only have eight days to go home, and I couldn't believe it, but he was right. I went on to work and I already bought some nice clothes, so I am thankful for that. I told my boss I would have to leave in a week, and he said, "Don't worry. We will always have a place for you here.", and I said thank you. They were all nice to me. I will continue to work until the last day before leaving. We all get along well, and I have kept the boys and they got to go out in the evenings. I'm already leaving but I have to go to my last school and that will be good.

Today is my last day of work, and my uncle will be taking me home tomorrow. All the people from the restaurant gave me ten dollars apiece, so I had a total of eighty dollars from the workers and the boss; that was so kind of them. I had to tell them I wouldn't be coming back, and they wished me peace and happiness.

My aunt cooked us a good dinner and made us a strawberry pie for dessert. My uncle said we will have to be up at five a.m. and leave at six because he was in the dry good business and had made appointments with motels and hotels to sell draperies to, so he could make money on the way home.

I had all my clothes together and uncle had his, so he packed them in his car that night so we could leave quicker. My aunt didn't let the kids up because she said they would be crying. We were up soon as the clock alarmed and my aunt made coffee and she still had strawberry pie left and cut us a piece, and my uncle said we had to go. I thanked my aunt for everything, and she thanked me for helping her with the kids. We hugged each other and we were on our way. It was still dark but beginning to break day and we liked that. Uncle said we can stop in Lexington, KY and eat lunch at a really good restaurant he always stopped at when he was on the road, and he said everyone liked it.

I was anxious to get home and see my family. I will only have two weeks at home, and I will have to go to Lexington for the rest of my schooling and then I will go to Michigan for a job.

My uncle was driving a little fast because he has his appointments made in Lexington and he will need to be there on time.

"LEXINGTON"

We have finally arrived in Lexington and Uncle is taking us to the good restaurant he talks about; it was pretty on the outside and looked new. We went in and they had really nice booths and the waitress seated us. They had a large menu and I ordered fried chicken, mashed potatoes and green beans. Uncle ordered fish and chips and coleslaw. Everything looked good when she brought it over and when I tasted it, it was delicious; now I know why everyone called it good. He asked me to get a small bite of the fish on his plate at the edge and I tasted it. I do not know which was better, the chicken, or the fish. I told him I would pay for our lunch, but he wouldn't let me. That was a very nice restaurant and I hope I can remember where it is at. We were soon back on the road and our next stop was my home. We were getting anxious. He said we should be at mom and dad's home in about two hours. We began to see the mountain peaks and it was a little scary to me because I had to live in those mountains, and it was difficult and frightening when the mining strikes came. I will never forget it. We are now on the highway to mom and dad's house. It's about three miles, and uncle said we are almost there. We went around a big curve, and I could see the house. We soon pulled up to the little grocery store gas station. Dad was pumping gas for someone, and we pulled in and he was happy to see us. My mom was happy to see us, and she had prepared a big dinner for us, and my uncle loved her cooking; he really loved the mountains, but he had his appointments, and he couldn't stay and would have to leave early in the morning. Our uncle didn't have time to socialize. He was very grateful for the good dinner mom made. My brother next to me will graduate next year and he is wanting to go into the Army, but dad is hoping he will change his mind, and mom, too. My uncle told him, "You are too smart to do that." So, maybe he will listen to him. Mom told my uncle she would make him lunch in the morning, but he told her he wants to go back to the good restaurant he always goes back to; so, she said OK, and he said all he wants is a cup of coffee because he had eaten too much at dinner. He asked mom to set the clock for him and he put it beside the bed he would sleep in. He was really tired with all that driving and will be working tomorrow, also. Mom and I cleaned up the kitchen and we all went into the living room to talk and discuss things and we were all tired. My little sister and brother are happy kids and have grown a few inches this past couple of months. I was happy to see them; they are always good. We all were enjoying talking with each other, but uncle was going to sleep. Mom said we all better get to bed because uncle must sleep because he will have to drive home after his work. We all went to bed.

The next morning, I heard the clock going off in the bedroom uncle was in, at five a.m. I got up and mom was perking coffee for him, and she told me not to wake the other kids up and I didn't. Uncle was washing his face and hands. He went into the kitchen and still looked very tired. Mom poured him some coffee and he used cream, and he said it tasted good. Dad got up and came into the kitchen and mom poured him some coffee and he looked tired, also. We were all talking low so the kids wouldn't get up. Uncle finished his coffee and put his dress white shirt on and a sport jacket; he always dressed good and looked nice working. He was the top dry good salesman for Michigan dry goods, and they liked him. He said, "I have to get going now." Dad shook his hand and said to be careful. Mom and I hugged him, and I thanked him for my stay with them while I worked. We all liked him a lot. He headed to his car with his suitcase. We were sad to see him go. I made myself a cup of cocoa and it was really good. We were sitting at the table, and I told mom and dad I only have eleven days to stay home because I will have to get checked in at the school and the place I will stay in Lexington. I told them I would call them and sometimes write a letter to the kids. Mom had my scholarship put away and I told her to get it out and she got it and said put it in the top chest of drawers until I'm ready to go, and I did. We sat at the kitchen table until eight a.m. and I heard the kids getting up. They asked where our uncle was and mom told them he was going back home, and they wanted to know when he would come back and mom said we didn't know, but he will call us, and your aunt will write to you; so, they were happy. Mom made them some cocoa and pancakes and they loved that, and dad had some pancakes and another coffee. Then he went up and opened the gas station grocery store and mom stayed with us. It was Saturday and they were happy to be home. The kids asked me when I would go to Lexington, and I told them in about two weeks. They know I will have to leave, and they don't want me to leave again.

The kids are counting the days until I leave. Mom said they will be upset, but they know I'm going to school. Dad asked if I wanted him to take me to school and I said, "No, I will take the bus to Lexington." He had to be retired from the mines because he has "rock dust" in his lungs, also called silicosis, medically. He is really skinny because he doesn't eat well and coughs a lot. They said he might get a little better, but we don't know. Time will tell. My little sister wants me to stay home, but she knows I can't do that. My younger brother says he wants me to stay home with them, the brother next to me said you have to do what's best for you; that's the best answer I heard from him. I will do that, I told him. Tomorrow I will have ten days left. They are counting the days and the younger two will start crying when I leave. I asked dad if all of us could go to the drive-in restaurant and I would buy it for us, and he said he will buy it for us, and we will go tomorrow evening. Mom has a lot of food left over that she cooked for our uncle, and she wants us to eat it tonight and we will; everything is good. I asked dad if we could go to town after we ate, and he said yes. He must close the little store first, then we could go. I hurried up and cleaned the kitchen up and dad closed the store, and we were all ready. I wanted to look at the little town. It's a lot smaller than Lexington and only has a few stores; and I'm a bit emotional about it.

I asked dad to drive slowly; I wanted to look at all the stores and he went very slow. I was looking at all the stores and thinking how many times I had been in them. I dread leaving my little brother and sister. They get very emotional. We were already told we would get one week off for Christmas and New Years, and one week off for the fourth of July. We also worked weekends for doctors and lawyers watching their children. We got free food from the cafeteria for the first two months and after that we earned our money for food. We also had to save money to catch the bus home if our parents didn't pick us up. Time went really fast, and we got our diplomas, and I went home for a week and had enough money to pay for my bus ticket to Michigan.

My time is ticking fast; I have four days until I catch the bus and dad will drive me to Harlan so I will leave from there.

The next morning, me and mom got up at five a.m. and I helped her iron all the kids' clothes before they got up for school. They got on the school bus, and we ate breakfast after they went to school. I told dad, "You know you have to drive me to Harlan in the morning", and he said, "Yes". I've got my big suitcase packed and my extra shoes are in it and my scholarship. I told dad to drive me to Harlan before they got up in the morning and he said yes, so we have everything under control and no crying.

It was evening and mom made dinner and everyone ate. I cleaned up the kitchen for mom. She was tired. She told all the kids to hurry up and take a bath and they were quick. They wanted to sit up a while and mom said OK. They were getting tired of talking and one by one they hugged me and said wake us up in the morning and I said I will try, but mom doesn't like to see them cry.

The next morning, dad put my suitcase in the car, and I had my shoes in a plastic bag to carry with me. I hugged mom and kissed her on the cheek, and I got in the car. We headed down the road. It took about forty-five minutes, and I carried my purse, and dad carried my suitcase in. I checked in and hugged dad and kissed him on the cheek and the lady said they will be boarding for Lexington. I said, "Thank you", and sat down with the Lexington group. Dad was a little sad but didn't look back. He still coughs a lot from the coal dust, but they didn't say he would get well.

I fell asleep on the bus; I was tired. The bus driver announced we were fifteen minutes from Lexington, so I wanted to stay awake so I could get off the bus quickly. I will still have to catch a taxi and go to the address where I will be staying, check in there, and give them my scholarship to copy. They explained to me that we could eat free for two months and then we would have to babysit for doctors and lawyers to pay for our food after that. That was fine for me, and I wasn't lazy, so I worked for food. It wasn't a problem. Everyone got settled. The time was flying after we settled in. We were busy all the time and working on Friday and Saturday and in school all week. We really got tired sometimes. They kept us busy with lots of homework. We were allowed to make one phone call a week and I called mom and dad.

Time has flown by, and I get to go home for Christmas in another week. I have really good grades in school, and everyone is nice, I will be getting my bus tickets Saturday morning for each way. I don't want dad to have to drive me back to Lexington; he still has to cough a lot. All of us are talking about how time is passing fast; we are kept busy. We have a lot of classes, and we are on the run a lot.

It is now two more days before I will be going back home. We have had all our tests, and I did very well with them. We are all tired from studying. One of the house mothers asked me if everything was OK with my family and I said yes; I think she seen how tired I was when I came back from home this time from worrying about my brother. Our whole family was very worried. I have to get my bus tickets this evening and

I will be leaving for home in the morning. I got tickets for leaving and coming back. That's what we all do. Very few parents could come to pick their children up. Not many women drove cars and the men worked different shifts and that made it difficult. Mom and dad said they are going to move out of the mountains soon as the kids are all out of school. I sure hope he can live long enough to do that for mom.

I have to get up at six a.m. and be at the bus station at seven to check in. Most of us have to do that, but we all have to call a taxi to take us to the bus station. We are happy that we are going home at Christmas. We told each other to have a good Christmas and the taxis were lined up and we were on our way.

We were all living in different areas, some were two hundred miles away and others one hundred. They came from all the coal mining areas in the Appalachians. We were mostly all poor, but we all loved our families. I was really tired, and I finally fell asleep, and the bus driver said we are in Corbin right now. He woke me up. He said the next stop would be Harlan, so I tried to stay awake, but it was hard. We were turning into the Harlan bus station and people were standing up and getting their suitcases overhead and I was a little slow, but I got it. I looked for dad's car but couldn't see it at first. Finally, I saw it. All the cars were crowded up because of Christmas. Dad seen me and he pulled up as far as he could. He got out of the car, and I hugged him, and he put the suitcase in the car. We quickly got out of the crowded bus station and was going home, and he said, "Your brother (the next one under me), joined the Army." I said, "Why didn't you tell me?" He said, "Your mom said not to, that she would tell you." We are worried because a war could break out at any time. We must hope for the best. I can't believe how warm it is, about sixty degrees. I don't even have to wear a coat. We were talking and dad almost passed the house up. He had to back up. My little sister came running to me and she wanted to help me carry my suitcase, but I told her it was too heavy. So, I took it into the house myself and dad went in the grocery store and mom came out and came down to the house and she told younger brother to come in the house with us and he said, "Are you going to stay a few days?", and I said, "Yes", and he smiled. Mom had already been cooking for Christmas and I hadn't bought anyone a gift, but I gave my brother and little sister five dollars, and they were happy.

No one will be with us this Christmas. The eldest brother and his wife will be going to her family reunion and the older brother next to me joined the Army and our other brother is trying his best to hold a job down and keep his sanity, and we will be lonely. We will miss all of them. We just have to make the best of everything.

Mom is still praying that our brother will find his daughter, and we are all hoping he will. Dad still has that rock dust cough, and we worry about that. We just had to ask him if he would drive us to our little town to see the Christmas lights and he said yes, and we were all ready to go. Our small town looked good at night with the Christmas lights. We asked if we could come back tomorrow and eat at our favorite restaurant and dad said yes. We were all happy. We were on our way home and mom said we could have some chicken. She broiled it in the oven and flavored it well, and she stuffed it, and it was a big hen. It was really good, we all loved it. She also baked a ham, but it wasn't as big as the hen and dad and mom usually liked it, but they didn't want any tonight. We all finished eating and there weren't many dishes, so I told mom to go sit with dad in the living room and I cleaned the kitchen up and put everything away, and she thanked me for it.

The next day, we all went to the restaurant. We all love their pies; nobody can beat them! They are excellent! We stayed up a little longer tonight, talking about our brother, Mary, and their daughter. He is so depressed because his wife was murdered, and he can't find his daughter. God only knows how he felt. We didn't really know; it was as if he lost himself and none of us could help him. It was as if he were running away from it but couldn't get away from it. He was still crying when he talked to us. Mom has said many a prayer that he can find his daughter and we all want that. Mom said we have to change the subject, or the kids will be crying.

We have two more days until Christmas and the kids have a lot of packages under the tree. They will be happy to open them. I don't think mom and dad bought toys for younger brother and little sister; they are growing up fast. Mom says my younger brother will be in high school next year, it doesn't seem like it!

I only have two days to get back to school. Dad will have to drive me to the bus station early on the second morning. Tomorrow is Christmas and the kids will open their gifts and that will make them happy. I told them to not get me anything and I meant it. Mom and dad always bought clothes for each other and that's all they care about. I will catch the bus back to school the morning after Christmas. Dad told me not to worry, he will be up early the day I go back. I said OK. The kids got to bed early because they wanted to be up first thing in the morning. Mom said she is not going to wake them in the morning; she's sure they will be up before us. We were all tired, so we all went to bed.

The next morning, I heard the kids laughing. They were stacking up the presents with their names on them and I heard mom getting up and she washed her hands and face and tied her hair up and started frying bacon. I told the kids to wait until dad gets up to open the gifts. They said OK. Dad was the last one to get up. He told the kids to start opening their gifts and they were fast opening them.

I had seen mostly clothes and shoes. They were happy and they started trying on clothes, and it looked like everything fit them. They were happy. Mom told all of us to come to the table, and we did. She made us cocoa, and we were happy; her and dad drank coffee. The kids were telling mom they liked their clothes and mom said, "Good. I won't have to take any back." Mom and dad opened their gifts and dad got two pairs of dress pants and a white shirt and a blue one. He was happy. Mom got a dress and a skirt and a blouse, and dad handed me a gift, and it was chocolate candy. I said thank you, and we were all happy. We didn't have all the family with us, but we were happy; but we missed the rest of the family. After breakfast was over, mom and I cleaned up the kitchen. We all relaxed and enjoyed the day with each other, as I had to leave in the morning.

"BACK TO LEXINGTON"

Dad was up and mom was in the kitchen frying bacon. She told me to close the bedroom doors so they wouldn't smell the bacon and I did. I think they were tired because they got up so early yesterday. Mom doesn't want them crying when I leave, and I understand. Mom had all the plates on the table, so she told me and dad to sit down and we ate bacon and scrambled eggs, and I had cocoa and they had coffee. Dad and I ate fast, and he washed his hands when he got up from the table and got my suitcase and put it in the car, and I got my leather bag and put my shoes in it. I kissed mom on the cheek and told her bye and to tell brother and sister I love them. She said she would. Dad said, "Let's go, you don't want to be late." I said, "No, I don't." So, we were on our way to the bus station. I was somewhat anxious to get back to school, I just want the time to be fast. I want to get through all of it and go back to Michigan and get a job and live there. My aunt and uncle still live there, and my grandparents live there now, also. So, I will have family there. Dad said we will be at the bus station in ten minutes. Time went fast while we were talking.

I seen the bus station lights and dad was pulling over by the doors and he parked a little way down and he got my suitcase out of the car, and I had my purse and leather bag. He walked me through the doors, and we went to the counter, and I got checked in and gave them my tickets. It wasn't crowded at all. I told dad I loved him, thanked him and kissed him on the cheek, and he walked back to the doors. I'm concerned that he has lost weight, but mom says he's OK. I was happy to get on the bus and get settled so I could sleep some before I have to get off. I'm tired from being with the family. The children stayed right with me, and they kept me busy. They were still sweet but growing up fast. They knew I wouldn't be back for a long time, and they are missing our brother that joined the Army. They are lonely with us gone.

I went to sleep quick, and I woke up hearing the bus driver saying we will be unloading the bus in fifteen minutes; we will be in Lexington. I was a little excited, but I also knew we would be given a lot of work to do. They really push us, and we have respect for them.

My time at school was going fast. I called mom and dad and told them I was getting out of school for Easter, and I would go see them. Dad was still coughing a lot and she didn't want him to drive.

I am tired of studying; one more night and our studies are over, and we will know our grades before we leave for Easter week.

It's Friday morning and we are in the study room, and they will be giving out our test papers. We were waiting and the Administrator was passing out our papers and I was the second person to get mine. I was happy I got one hundred percent right, so I have an A+, you can't get better than that! I really worked for it!

I have to get my clothes ready because I will be taking the bus home in the morning. I went home for the break and returned to Lexington for school. I went in and checked myself in and one of the house mothers was there and she asked if I had seen all my family and I said yes. She said several of the girls came in today and went to their rooms to sleep; they were tired. I said, "I'm going to do the same." I laid down and left my suitcase by my bed and was awakened by my roommate taking her clothes out and hanging them in the closet, so I got up and hung mine up. We all had twin beds and we liked that.

"BACK TO SCHOOL"

We got up early and went to the cafeteria to eat. The house mother said they have several babysitting jobs open for Friday and Saturday, and I agreed to work both evenings and she was asking the other girls to work also, and they agreed. That's how we paid for our food.

We have three months until we graduate, and I will leave for Michigan. All of us are going to different places for work. We will be happy to work. Time is going fast.

We will be having testing for the next two weeks and we must study hard. When we watch peoples' children, we will have to take the books with us and study as much as possible. Most people tell us to have the children in bed at nine p.m. The people usually come home by twelve. They are professional people and visit friends on the weekends. We will be through studying this Friday, and testing will be next week. We are all ready to graduate next Friday.

Our graduation is over, and we are all happy. We are all thanking our house mothers; they were good to us, and they wished us well. I had my suitcase and leather bag ready to go to Michigan.

I must be back in Michigan on Tuesday. I have a good job interview at three p.m. My uncle said he will take me to Michigan and hopefully, my aunt can get me to my interview. She said she could. I had to work fast and make sure my aunt took me there. My aunt had dinner fixed upon our arrival. My uncle knows a man that said he just fixed a fifty-six Ford up and will sell it cheap to me. We will look at it tomorrow morning.

The next morning, we went to look at the Ford. I liked it and bought it. I went to my interview, and I got the job! Things seem to be going really well for me, so far.

A month or so went by and a male coworker friend of mine introduced me to a guy named Joe. Joe was just full of smiles and asked if he could take me out sometime. I told him I didn't know him well enough. He said we would see each other around and that one day we would go out. He made sure that I seen him and started getting to know him. We finally went out to dinner one night. I told him that I would pay for my dinner, and he would not let me. He took me back to my aunt's and we all talked for a while. They really liked him. Joe had moved to Michigan for a better job and is staying with his grandmother.

I like my job and my supervisor. I am going to look for an apartment near my work. I have to look for an apartment on my days off. I will be off Thursday and Friday this week, so I washed my clothes at my aunt's house and dried and ironed them. My aunt had a little paper that had apartment rentals in it, and she said I could look in it and I found two near where I work and will see them today. My aunt's phone was ringing, and she said, "It's Joe." I said, "I didn't give him the number." She said she did, that he asked for it. I said, "I didn't know that." Anyway, I talked to him and told him I have two appointments to look at them and he asked if he could go with me to see them and I said, if he wanted to. I said, "One's at four p.m. and one's at five p.m." He said, "I can go. I get off at three thirty." I said, "OK." He said, "I will pick you up." I said, "OK." My aunt said he is a nice guy and good looking. I said, "I know; he has been doing everything for me." My aunt said, "He keeps an eye on you. I think he is a keeper."

My aunt was getting things together for dinner. Her husband will be home at five p.m., and her two boys at three thirty, from school. I helped peel potatoes and make a big salad. I saw the school bus out front, and she said, "The boys are coming home." I really liked them; they were nice.

Next thing we heard was a horn toot out front. I have to go right now to see the four o'clock apartment. It's about a half mile from here. My aunt said it's fifteen minutes until four. I had the paper in my hand with the address of the apartments and Joe drove me straight to the place. I knocked on the door and an older woman opened it and I said, "I called you. I want to see the apartment." She walked to the side of her house and opened the door, and it only had a stove and fridge, and it smelled like beer, and I said, "What's that smell?" She said, "I don't know." I said, "I can't take this one with no washer or dryer." We left and Joe said that some drunk must have gotten thrown out.

We went to the next one and it had everything and was very clean. I asked how much the rent was, and it was cheaper than the other one. I said, "I will take it, but I will have to give you the money tomorrow." She said that was fine. Joe said it was a good deal and closer to my work.

We went back to my aunt's, and she was putting dinner on the table and my uncle just walked in the door and she had set plates for us, and Joe told her he wanted to take me to the place I had worked at to eat; but my aunt said it's free here and we agreed to eat with them. Joe asked me why I had left Michigan and I told him I had to, as I had got a scholarship and had to go to school. I told him that Michigan pays better and that's why I came back. He said, "Good. I'm happy to hear that because I'm staying in Michigan." I asked him where he worked, and he said he was in a tool factory, and he was saving his money and going to a small college. I told him, "You should get in with Ford or GM, and they will pay for your education." He said he may try that.

Joe and I thanked them, and we cleaned up the table and rinsed the dishes and put them in the dishwasher. My aunt thanked us. My uncle said, "Come in the living room and sit with us", and we did. Joe stayed a bit and left. His grandmother keeps tabs on him.

I had moved to the apartment I found, and Joe said he would pay my rent and I said no; and he said yes, and he asked if I would go to a nice restaurant with him. I said yes, but it would have to be Saturday when I was off from work. He said OK. He came over on Saturday evening and I dressed up and he wore a white shirt and black pants. He took me to a nice restaurant, and they were playing nice music. We had ordered our food and he looked over at me and said, "I want you to be my wife." I said, "Let me think on that and give me until tomorrow." He said, "OK. Can I see you tomorrow?" I said yes. We sat for about an hour talking about things and the future, and we both had some of the same ideas. We had a lot in common and we both knew that.

He drove me back to my apartment and said, "You will have an answer for me tomorrow, right?" I said, "Yes." He gave me my first kiss and a big hug, and he said, "I'll see you about one o'clock." I said OK.

The next day he was at the door at five minutes to one o'clock and he said, "What is the answer?" I said, "Yes." He hugged me and said, "I wanted to ask you that the second time I saw you, but I was afraid to. I thought you would think I was crazy."

Joe had bought rings for me the next day after I said yes, and I had to buy him one, and I did. He asked me, "Do you want a minister to marry us?" I said, "No." He said, "Is a Justice of the Peace, OK?" I said, "Yes." We each had to get a witness and we did, and I was a bit nervous, but Joe was very happy. When he put my rings on and I put his on, I was still a little nervous but got over it. He moved into the apartment with me. We progressed very well saving money and bought several houses together throughout the years. We had two daughters. We were happy.

The years went on and my brother Pippy was still searching for his daughter. I had talked to my brothers in Ohio; we all did, and they were seemingly OK, but our eldest brother Herby called dad, and mom said he had had a sad look on his face, and she asked him what was wrong. He said, "Wait, and I will tell you." Herby, the eldest brother, said Pippy's doctor had put him on sedatives, and he had been nervous and could not stop looking for his daughter and he is still looking and can't get over the death of Mary, it has drove him crazy. His hands are shaky, and he is scared and nervous and has messed his life up. Only God knows how he is feeling. He got involved with the wrong group of men and left a hotel after meeting up with them. The Feds had the room wire tapped and were listening in on them. He left and was transporting a million dollars' worth of counterfeit money and jewelry when he was pulled over by State Troopers. They asked him to open his trunk and found all of it. They knew exactly where it was. He was arrested and taken to jail. He would not tell who was involved with it. This has hurt all of us. We are all nervous and waiting for a call from our eldest brother Herby for updates. He is supposed to pay a bondsman and they will let him out until his trial. We can hardly believe this, but it's real.

My eldest brother called dad this morning and said he will have to take a day off to take our older brother with him and the bondsman before the judge and they will release him on bond until he has a court date. He had never been in court, that we know of, except when Mary was killed, and they had him in the jail. The older brother said when they let him out, he can call dad.

We are awaiting a call from my older brother. Finally, Herby called. The judge seen our brother and he's out of jail and he wanted to speak to dad. I spoke to him when he called me, and I told him Joe and I would try to come see him, but we didn't know where he would be yet. I got off the phone in tears. I felt so bad for him, but he didn't know I was crying.

They called and told me my favorite brother was in court and the judge sentenced him to four years in prison for the crime he was charged with. He went to prison in Leavenworth, Kansas. Mom said he is still looking for his daughter; he will never stop, we know that. He has some people he knows in Ohio that wrote letters to people in different states that told them his daughter's age and when she was born and what age she would be now, hoping he could track her somehow, but it never happened. He lost his job when they sent him to prison, so he will have to find another one when he gets out and still will be looking for his daughter. He has been so broken since all this happened.

I am worried about my mom. She had such a bad life with her dad and a hard life with my dad. It seems like her life didn't have much happiness in it. I'm still praying my brother will find his daughter and so is my mom. She hopes it will be before she dies.

Pippy was good to us, and we don't know how he got tangled up with those people. He got with the wrong people and did what they told him to do, but he was on pills for his nerves and stressed out over all of this and all the things that happened to him.

God knows he had never done anything bad or been in prison. He was so torn up when his wife was murdered and then found out his sister-in-law turned the baby in to the Catholic Orphanage, is what we were told. We didn't know what to do when he had gone to jail being accused of the murder. We all panicked. That was one of the hardest days in our lives.

Joe and I had planned the trip to go see Pippy. We left early in the morning and travelled until we needed gas. He seen a gas station and stopped to fill up the car and asked if I needed to use the bathroom. We both used the bathroom, and we quickly were back on the road. I told him I was sleepy, and he told me to reach in the backseat and get the cushion and I put it by my head, and I was leaning on the door. I fell asleep and woke up an hour later and he said, "We are fifty-two miles from Leavenworth." I said, "You must have been flying", and he laughed. It was almost eleven a.m. We were going up the steps and it was a huge building, an old dark brick and very big and tall. It looked like an old church in the front but was really long going back. We finally got to the top of the steps, and he opened the door, and we walked in and there was a man at the desk. He looked like a captain of a police force, and he said, "Who are you here to see?" I told him, "My brother." He asked for his name, and he went through the alphabetical log, and he said, "No one is here by that name." I told him that I write letters to him here all the time. Then he asked, "What did he do?" I said, "He was in his car and was pulled over by a policeman and he had a suitcase full of a million dollars in counterfeit money, and a lot of jewelry, and he was taken to jail for that." The man told us, "He is over there in that building with all the executives" and laughed. So, we left and there was a field of buffalo beside the building, and we went in and a man at the desk said he was there. I turned around and seen him, and started running to him, and the man said, "Ma'am, you have to sign in before you can talk to him." I went back and told him I was sorry. He said, "That's OK. I know you were excited, but we have to have your ID and you have to sign your name before you can talk to him." So, I signed in and Joe had to sign in also. We went to sit down at a table to talk. We were happy to see each other. Joe and he took a liking to each other when they first met years ago. He thanked Joe for us coming to see him. The man said we could only be there with him for two hours because they have a lot of people coming in.

Joe's mother lived beside an onion ring factory that also had mushrooms breaded and fried there, and there was a man in trouble with the IRS that ran that place and was going to prison. He had given Joe's mom several Spanish pictures and she gave them to Joe. We gave them to my mom and dad, and they had them on their wall, as they matched their Spanish furniture. Joe's mom told him the man's name and he asked my brother in prison about him, and he said, "He is our cook!" Joe asked if we could meet him, and he came out and my brother said, "Your pictures are on my dad's wall", and it was explained to him. What a coincidence!

We asked if there was anything we could get him, or send him and he said, "No. I'm happy to see you." The man that let us in came over and said our time was up and I hugged my brother and kissed him on his cheek and told him I loved him, and he said the same to me. He and Joe shook hands and we left.

We were going to head on and visit mom and dad. We were just leaving the prison and Joe asked me to get the map. He said we will go through Missouri a different way and it will border Kentucky, and we will go right into Kentucky, and we can drive toward your parents' home. He said we probably wouldn't get there until dark, and I said, "That's alright." He told me when I see a gas station to pull in and we can use the bathroom and get some gas. I said OK; and I drove about a mile and stopped at a small gas station. The man that ran the gas station came out and asked, "How much you want?" Joe said, "Fill it up." Joe paid him and said he would drive now so I got in on the passenger side and he asked if I was hungry, and I said no. He said we needed to stop and get a hot dog, so we won't have my mom cooking at night. I said, "If we can have chili on it, that's fine." He said I will stop when I see a place. About three miles ahead was little drive in, and he pulled in and the car hop came up to the car and Joe rolled the window down and he ordered us a hot dog with chili and asked what I wanted to drink, and I said a Coke, and he ordered one also. When we finished our food, he sat the tray on the swing out table and left the girl a tip on it, and we were back on the road.

It was beginning to get a little dark and Joe said there's a big road sign ahead if you can read it and it said, "Harlan, twenty-two miles ahead." Joe was always amazed by the mountains. He said he had never been in them before marrying me. We are now seeing the little gas station grocery store that dad and mom run. The lights are on at it, and they will soon be closing and going down the sidewalk to the house.

We pulled in the gravel area and went into the little store. My dad and oldest brother were in the store, and they were asking me how our brother was doing, and I told them he had lost some weight, and his hands were still shaking some, and that he was still nervous and taking pills for his nerves in prison. Dad said he was closing the store and told us to go on down to the house, and Joe got our suitcases out and we knocked on the door and my younger brother said, "Come on in." He was happy to see me and so was my little sister. Mom came into the living room and thanked us for going to see Pippy. Dad and older brother came down to the house and we all were tired, but we talked for about an hour and went to bed.

The next morning, we were up early, and mom was cooking breakfast and she made homemade biscuits, eggs, bacon, gravy and fried potatoes, and she asked Joe if he wanted coffee, and he said yes. I told her I will make cocoa for me, and the kids and she said OK. Mom said we will all eat first, then we will wake the kids and let them eat, so they will be quiet when they are eating. She asked when we have to go back and I said, "We were planning to leave today." She asked, "Can you stay another day?" I said, "Joe, can we stay another day?" He said we could. I know he wants to see the mountains and dad said he can shoot guns with him and older brother; they have a target and can practice. I think Joe liked that idea, so we will leave tomorrow. I heard a noise in the bedroom. The kids are getting up and they can eat now. Mom told them I will leave tomorrow, and they were happy. I told mom she can go up to the store and open it and I will clean the kitchen up while the guys are target shooting and I'll help the kids with whatever they want to do; they are being nice. Mom said they may be selling the place and moving to London, and I said I hoped so. Mom always wanted out to a bigger town. She always said there's nothing for women to do in the mountains and she was right. The kids finished eating and I cleaned the kitchen up and went up to the store and kids went out and was watching the guy's target shooting.

I made the bed and straightened up the chairs in the living room and wiped the table good. I checked the bathroom, it was very clean and neat, so I got my good clothes on and went up to the store with mom. She asked what the kids were doing, and I said, "Watching them shoot the targets." I told mom I hope dad means it when he said he will move to London. She said, "I hope so, it's hard to get him out of the mountains. I said, "I know."

It wasn't long until the kids were tired of watching the target shooting and they came in the store and said dad is going to take older brother and Joe on top of the mountain and they wanted to go. They finally came up to the store and mom asked if I wanted to go with them, and I said, "Not really. I'll stay here if you want to go with them and leave the kids with me." Mom said for me to go with them and leave the kids here. She wanted me to see all the dogwood trees and the honey suckles blooming in the mountains and I said, "I will go." She knew I loved the blooming trees, and I asked if my little sister could go with us and she said yes, and she said that way her and her brother wouldn't be fighting. I said OK.

Dad and Herby, my eldest brother, were happy to take us to the top of the mountain. They liked the trees blooming too. We all got in the car, and we were on our way. Herby said he wished his wife could see the trees in bloom, but she stayed with her mother because she was sick. It took forty-five minutes to get to the top and we looked over the mountain into the valleys and everything was beautiful. The blooms were in different colors, but the dogwoods were white. We looked at everything and wished we had a camera but didn't have one. Dad asked if we were ready to go down and we said yes. We headed down and the curves were steeper and after about ten minutes, Joe said, "Stop the car!" He was nauseated and started vomiting and he was very embarrassed and had to take his handkerchief out and wipe his mouth. He told us all he was sorry, and dad said a lot of people get sick on the curvy roads and not to worry about it. We were soon back on the straight roads and soon we were home. I asked my older brother when he was going home, and he said tomorrow.

We were up real early, and mom had coffee made for Joe, older brother and her and dad. I made me a cup of cocoa and that was enough for me. I told Joe we needed to get out of here before the kids got up, or they would be crying. Older brother said, "That's true, they always cry." Joe put our clothes in the car and older brother put his in his car. I hugged mom and dad and kissed them on the cheek and older brother hugged them, too.

It's still dark and there are no streetlights in the mountains, and you have to dim your lights, or you will blind the other drivers. Joe picked up on that fast, years ago, when a car didn't dim their lights. He said, "It blinds you." I said, "I know."

We were having the road to ourselves after we left Harlan County. Not many cars were on the road, but it was still very dark. Joe asked if I wanted to stop and eat breakfast and I said, "If we found a place open", and he said OK. It was about ten miles before we seen anything, and we saw a big restaurant. We stopped and it was really clean and had nice booths and the coffee smelled good. We each ordered bacon and eggs and fried potatoes, and it was really good. Joe was reading the menu and said, "They have homemade pecan pie. Let's have a piece, and they will bring some more coffee." I had decaffeinated, so she brought some more, and the pie slices were big, and it was the best pecan pie I ever ate, and Joe loved it. We were out the door and back on the road. We loved that breakfast!

Moving fast forward, my brother got out of prison, and he was still very nervous and still looking for his daughter. One day, he got a phone call and the woman who called, called him by name and asked him if that was his name, and he said yes. She said, "Daddy." He said, "Are you, my daughter?" and she said, "Yes. I have been looking for you for a long time." He said, "I have looked for you since you were in the Catholic Orphanage. You were put there by your mom's sister." That's what the nuns had told him. They also said that she would have to find him, she was already adopted. He asked her, "Where are you at?" She said, "Oklahoma", and she gave him her address and he said he would be there soon. He was there the next day, and they both were crying. It was so emotional, and both had a lot of questions for each other. She said the family that adopted her had also adopted a baby boy, and that was her brother from another family. She said her dad worked at the Space Center and her mom was a nurse and she and the adopted brother were young teenagers when the mom and dad were killed in a car accident and their families put them away. The family of the mom and dad gave them some money and they ran the streets and got into some drugs and then quit them and then she started looking for him, she said.

She said she had his name and had looked all over the United States for him. Then, she looked to find him in Ohio because Ohio had people with that name, and she called them and finally found him on the phone. He called mom and mom said, "God answered my prayers." She was happy and called me. I was happy, too!

In the meantime, my brother called me and said my mom has been diagnosed with cancer of the stomach and it has metastasized to the liver, and I was very scared when I heard that. Joe said he would take me to see her immediately. He said, "Don't worry." He is very good to me, and I am fond of him. We now have this to worry about. At least she did get out of the mountains, and they moved to London, KY.

My brother was very happy about his daughter, but distraught over mom. He tried so hard to find her for "many years". His daughter passed away a few years later. The doctors said she lived the longest of anyone with Lou Gehrig's disease. We have pictures of her, and we really didn't get to see her, but talked to her on the phone. My brother wanted to drive her to see us, but she got sicker and wanted to stay home with her care giver. We were so sorry she couldn't travel.

After leaving the Appalachians and pursuing my career, I fulfilled my dream of never being without. The closeness with my family remained until they began to die off. I lost my mother in 1992, and my eighty-eight-and-a-half-year-old dad in 1993. The memories of the good times and the bad times inspired me to write this book in hopes and prayer that no child ever has to endure the environment I did growing up. Now, at 82 years old I have overcome it all, but I have never forgotten.

Printed in the United States
by Baker & Taylor Publisher Services